מסורה

ArtScroll Mesorah Series®

Rabbi Nosson Scherman / Rabbi Meir Zlotowitz

General Editors

LISTEN TO

by

Rabbi Yissocher Frand

Published by

Mesorah Publications, ltd

YOUR MESSAGES

*And other observations on
contemporary Jewish life*

FIRST EDITION
First Impression ... August 1999
Second Impression ... August 1999
Third Impression ... January 2001

Published and Distributed by
MESORAH PUBLICATIONS, LTD.
4401 Second Avenue / Brooklyn, N.Y 11232

Distributed in Europe by
LEHMANNS
Unit E, Viking Industrial Park
Rolling Mill Road
Jarrow, Tyne and Wear, NE32 3DP England

Distributed in Australia and New Zealand by
GOLDS WORLD OF JUDAICA
3-13 William Street
Balaclava, Melbourne 3183
Victoria Australia

Distributed in Israel by
SIFRIATI / A. GITLER
6 Hayarkon Street
Bnei Brak 51127
Israel

Distributed in South Africa by
KOLLEL BOOKSHOP
Shop 8A Norwood Hypermarket
Norwood 2196, Johannesburg, South Africa

ARTSCROLL SERIES®
LISTEN TO YOUR MESSAGES
© Copyright 1999, by MESORAH PUBLICATIONS, Ltd.
4401 Second Avenue / Brooklyn, N.Y. 11232 / (718) 921-9000 / www.aertscroll.com

---

ISBN:
1-57819-139-4 (hard cover)
1-57819-140-8 (paperback)

Typography by CompuScribe at ArtScroll Studios, Ltd.

Printed in the United States of America by Noble Book Press Corp.
Bound by Sefercraft, Quality Bookbinders, Ltd., Brooklyn N.Y. 11232

To my wife Nechama,

Any attempt to articulate my feelings of gratitude would ring hollow. But to someone who understands my silences as clearly as my words, I say a simple Thank You.

מכתב ברכה

אברהם פאם
RABBI ABRAHAM PAM
582 EAST SEVENTH STREET
BROOKLYN, NEW YORK 11218

בס"ד ה' מנ"א תשנ"ה — מנחם ציון ורונה ירושלים יבנון כרבלים!

הנה הכבוד מוהר"ר יעקב צדוק הכהן שליט"א מכין לבנוס ספר
תורה לעתרי, ורק מ' מאני לכתוב בדי כיכנ. ואני נושא לקרלאתי דרכ
לך, לאמרות מלב הרעיונתי, ומולא עתי, מעני כבודו כי יהנ קאנ...
הנה האתהר כבר נונצ לתבליה קטפרי הקדומים והכריצ'לנועתי קדת
והקפטה ואוסר, לרהים נעניס מהם ומשלפטם מהם.
יהנ שלצית עת קטפנו המכב ויקכל קתשונות מן כין מנקל צ'נ ב',
ויכבכ לנפשל מאמנותו חולצ לצבות עת הריח אוד רדות קטעים,
מתוק ברריונת כעלי ומנותת הנפש.
ומברכם, יצהק הכבן כעלף

Preface

SECOND BOOKS INEVITABLY INVITE COMPARISONS WITH their predecessors. How are they similar? How are they different? I still find it somewhat incredible to see my speeches in book form, and I thank the *Ribono Shel Olam* from the depths of my heart for this profoundly moving experience. I am also grateful to Him for blessing my first efforts in print with some measure of success and pray that He do the same for this, my second offering.

No second book can duplicate the special excitement of the first appearance in print, but in certain ways, working on this book has been a sweeter experience. It took a greater effort to pull together the material for this book and transform it from the spoken to the printed medium. It was a very stimulating and creative process, and I only hope that my readers are as pleased with the results as I am.

There is one fundamental similarity between this book and my first. As I stated in the Preface to my first book, I have presented few, if any, novel ideas to the reader. The same holds true for this book. Rather, what I have tried to accomplish in the speeches upon which my books are based is to articulate issues that I myself often face and that I know from conversations with others that they are also facing. To help them and myself, I have researched sacred sources and shared with the public those discoveries that have had the most impact on me. Hopefully, they would help others as well.

Many times, we feel something bothering us but we cannot quite put our finger on it. However, when we hear someone talk about it and express it, we instantly recognize it. "That's it!" we say to ourselves. Furthermore, even when we can pinpoint the thought or feeling, we sometimes feel isolated, as if we are the only ones dealing with these particular issues. It is, therefore, reassuring and comforting to know that we are not alone, that others also contend with similar struggles and ordeals.

One of the most gratifying sights for me as a speaker is to see people in the audience nodding their heads, suggesting to me that they know exactly what I am saying. Though I will not have the good fortune of watching as readers go through my book, I hope that in the privacy of their homes, they will exclaim, "That's it!" I hope that in the privacy of their homes, I will bring smiles to their lips and an occasional tear to their eyes.

In this light, the reader will understand why the essays in this book are conversational in tone. They began as conversations with my audiences and, before that, as conversations with myself. Many of the issues discussed in these pages are essentially personal introspections, and if it sometimes appears that I am giving *mussar*, it is primarily directed at myself.

It is not easy to transform a speech into a written work. Even the most moving speeches can fall flat when they are transcribed verbatim. Only a gifted artist can transfer the spoken word to the written form without losing the thoughts, feelings and passion that inspired the original. I was fortunate to have the assistance of such an artist in the person of Rabbi Yaakov Yosef Reinman, a brilliant writer who used his creative talents to preserve the tone and style in which these lectures were originally presented. To him I say, *yasher koach* and thank you.

Working with ArtScroll has been a pleasure both professionally and personally. Rabbi Meir Zlotowitz and Rabbi Nosson Scherman continue to make an indelible mark of historic proportions on the Jewish world. Learning in general and Daf Yomi in particular would not be what they are today without the contributions of ArtScroll.

Moreover, since the publication of my first volume I have gotten to know Rabbi Zlotowitz on a personal basis and I consider him a friend. Indeed, I often find myself the undeserving recipient of his kindness.

My sincerest thanks to the talented people at ArtScroll: Particularly, Rabbi Avraham Biderman, who served as my contact person, for his valuable guidance, as well as Mrs. Judi Dick, who read the book and offered many valuable insights and comments.

As I look back over the four years since the publication of my first book and contemplate what is different, I am grateful that some things have remained the same. I am grateful to the *Ribono Shel Olam* that we can share the joy of this new publication with my mother, Mrs. Adele Frand, and my mother-in-law, Mrs. Esther Blumenkrantz. May Hashem grant them good health and *nachas* in the years to come.

I consider myself doubly blessed in my association with Yeshivas Ner Yisrael in Baltimore. Not only do I have the special *zchus* to teach there, but it is also the place where I live with my family and where we raised our children. The individuals that make up this unique *makom Torah* are like my very own family. I would like to take this opportunity to express my appreciation to Rav Naphtali Neuberger *shlita* for all he has done for me and my family, for the Yeshivah and for all of *Klal Yisrael.* May Hashem grant him many more years of health and strength to carry on his *avodas hakodesh.*

Since the publication of my last book, my family has grown from a three-child family to a five-child family, *bli ayin hara.* And no, my wife has not had twins. The *Ribono Shel Olam* in His kindness has answered our *tefillos* and given us two wonderful new children and a grandchild. Our daughter Avigayil married Yisroel Rapps, son of Mr. and Mrs. Dennis Rapps, and they have been blessed with a precious little girl, Malka. Our son Yakov married Shulamis Teichman, the daughter of Rabbi and Mrs. Heshie Teichman. We hope and pray that our son Baruch Yair, who was really the impetus for this book, will be as fortunate in his *zivug* as his siblings have been in theirs.

Katonti mikal hachasadim. I feel humbled by the many kindnesses that the *Ribono Shel Olam* has shown us in our lives, and I offer up my *tefillos* that He continue to do so in the future. In this month of Av, when thoughts of *geulah* occupy our minds, let me offer a *tefillah* that my wife and I, together with our family and all of *Klal Yisrael,* will greet *Mashiach bimheirah beyameinu. Amein.*

Yissocher Frand
Menachem Av 5759
Baltimore, Maryland

Table of Contents

PERSONAL GROWTH

Listen to
Your Messages

T HE CHIDDUSHEI HARIM ONCE NOTICED THAT ONE OF
his *chassidim*, a man who was ordinarily very outgo-
ing and exuberant, seemed strangely depressed.
"Why are you so downcast today?" the Chiddushei HaRim
asked him. "Why do you look so despondent?"

"I get depressed every summer," the man replied.

"But why?" asked the Chiddushei HaRim. "Is it the heat?"

"No, it's not the heat," said the man. "It's the *parshios
hashavua* of the summer. In *Behaaloscha*, we read about the
misonenim. In *Shelach*, we read about the *meraglim*. In
Korach, we read about Korach's rebellion. In *Chukas*, we
read about the *be'er*. In *Balak*, we read about the orgies at
Shittim. What is going on? What is happening to *Klal Yisrael*?
From *parshah* to *parshah*, we see them literally deteriorating. Why? What is wrong?"

Not many Jews today would get depressed about what happens in the *parshios hashavua*, but there once were such people in the world. Still, even if we do not quite get depressed about these questions, they still need to be addressed. Why indeed did *Klal Yisrael* go into a period of decline in the wilderness?

Some of the commentators explain that all these eruptions took place because of the Jewish people's inability to deal with change. They led a charmed life in the wilderness. Every morning, manna fell from the heavens and landed on their doorsteps. Their clothes never wore out. They lived in a virtual cocoon, protected by a pillar of cloud and a pillar of fire. And what awaited them in *Eretz Yisrael*? A normal life of toil and commerce, a natural rather than a supernatural existence. How would they ever exist without Moshe Rabbeinu? How would they cope with the unknowns of the future? These thoughts intimidated and disoriented them, and they reacted inappropriately.

People don't like changes — not in their personal lives, not in their social lives, not in their religious lives. Once they achieve a certain comfort level in their lives, they don't want any changes to come along and disrupt the equilibrium of their existence.

Change is, of course, inevitable. In fact, the inevitability of change is one of the only unchanging features of life. Our children reach a certain age, our parents reach a certain age, everything seems to be under control, life is just running along, and we are satisfied. We can deal with things as they are. But then our children get older. They leave home and enter new phases. Our parents get older and encounter new situations. Things are changing, and we don't like it. We are afraid of it. We have become addicted to the narcotic of complacency. We like it comfortable and predictable. We like it the way it is.

Therefore, any agenda of self-improvement which requires a change in the way we live and do things will be vigorously resisted. People, for instance, will readily admit that *shemiras halashon* is a very important issue. They will readily admit that *lashon hara* is a terrible sin. But how easily can they stop themselves from speaking improperly? Not very easily at all. Why? Because it requires change. We have to change the way we talk, the way we think, the way we act, the way we relate to other people. We have to change, but our inertia doesn't let us change.

There is also another reason people are so resistant to change. Changing entails an admission of earlier error. When people change the way they do things, they are admitting that the way they did things before was wrong. And who wants to admit he was wrong?

Rabbi Zev Leff, formerly of Miami Beach and now living in *Eretz Yisrael*, was once giving a *shiur* in *Hilchos Shabbos* in his *shul* between Minchah and Maariv. The subject was the laws of *borer*, the Biblical prohibition to separate the "good" from the "bad" on *Shabbos*.

During the *shiur*, a man who never came to *shiurim* showed up. He had *yahrzeit* that night and he wanted the *amud* for Maariv. He had miscalculated and arrived at the *shul* a little too early, and found himself stuck listening to the *shiur*. He heard the *rav* speaking about taking the fish from the bones and the watermelon from the seeds rather than the other way around.

After the *shiur*, the man approached the *rav*.

"Everything you said tonight," he said, "it all wasn't true, you know."

"What are you talking about?" asked the *rav*.

"This *borer* business," said the man. "There is no such thing as *borer*. It just can't be. You see, I am a *shomer Shabbos*, my father's a *shomer Shabbos*, and my grandfather was a *shomer Shabbos*. And I tell you, never ever did we hear about this thing called *borer*. It must be some kind of custom that some communities have, but it can't be the law."

Incredible, isn't it? The man could not face up to admitting that there had been an error in his family for generations. And if we think about it, don't we all act the same way when faced with something new? Aren't we also resistant to change? Would we find it easy to admit that what our fathers and mothers taught us was not right?

Rabbi Leff then made the very interesting observation that this man's defense mechanism is actually explained by a *passuk* in the Torah (*Vayikra* 26:14-15): "But if you will not listen to Me, and you will not perform all these commandments, if you reject My statutes, and you find My laws repugnant." Rashi explains that this is a chain reaction. If you refuse to learn, you won't perform. And if you don't perform, you will reject others who do perform. And if you reject those who perform, you will eventually despise the sages as well.

How clearly we see this happening. If a person refuses to learn about *borer*, for instance, he will certainly not fulfill this commandment. But that's not enough. It doesn't stop there. He looks around in the *shul*. He sees everyone else learning about *borer*, and he is upset. Now all his friends will be keeping the prohibition of *borer*, except for him. So how does he deal with it? He disparages them. They're just a bunch of right-wingers, a bunch of closet black-hatters. It is a difficult thing to do, but how else will he justify his own refusal to change his ways? How else will he rationalize to himself why he refuses to do what everyone else is doing? So he has to reject his more observant friends. It might not stop there, either. He is not doing it, and they are doing it. Who's responsible for all this trouble? The *rav*, of course. He is the one who is always on everyone's case, making trouble and refusing to leave well enough alone. And so that man begins to despise the *rav*.

Look where a simple refusal to change might lead this man. He can't admit that his upbringing was deficient, so he ignores his obligations, disparages his friends and despises his *rav*. All because he doesn't want to change.

Contrast this with the following story about a woman in Houston, Texas, a sincere woman who keeps Shabbos and a kosher home. She invites a religious couple for Shabbos, and they arrive not more than an hour before candle-lighting time with a gift for the hostess.

The woman opens the package and sees a stunning serving tray.

"Oh, it's beautiful!" she exclaims. "Thank you so much. We'll use it tonight in honor of Shabbos."

"Oh, I'm so sorry," says her guest. "We weren't able to *toveil* the tray, so you won't be able to use it on Shabbos."

"*Toveil?*" says the hostess. "What's that?" "You know," says the guest, "taking the dishes to a *mikveh* and immersing them in the water. You can't use them before you are *toveil* them."

"No, I didn't know," says the hostess. "Really? Is that what you're supposed to do? I've never *toiveled* anything in my life. My mother never told me about such a thing. But if that's what has to be done, I guess we won't be using your beautiful tray tonight."

The guest is struck by a sudden thought. "Wait a minute. Are you saying that all your dishes have never been *toiveled?*"

"I'm afraid so," says the hostess. "Oh my, what are we going to do?"

"Do you have any disposable dishes?" asks the guest.

"What an excellent idea!" says the hostess. "Of course I do. But what about the pots and pans with all the food? Don't they have to be *toveiled?*"

"Yes, they certainly do. Do you have any disposable aluminum pans and some foil?"

And so one half-hour before Shabbos, they transferred all the food into aluminum pans, and they ate from disposable dishes that whole Shabbos.

Now what would that gentleman who never heard of *borer* have done in this situation? Would he have responded as this hostess did? Or would he have insisted that this *toveiling* business is probably some kabbalistic custom which is not mandatory?

Change is a difficult thing. If you ask most American *rab-banim*, even in the best of congregations, to identify the most serious problem they face with their congregants, most will tell you that it is getting people to accept changes. After all, they learn Daf Yomi, send their children to the finest schools and come to *shul* three times a day. What more could you possibly want from them? They just want to be left alone.

Most people are guilty of an extremely serious sin which the Torah (*Devarim* 29:18) describes as, "*Shalom yihyeh li ki beshrirus libi eilech.*" Loosely translated, it means, "I'm fine. Leave me alone." The Chazon Ish calls someone who displays this attitude a *beinoni beshitah*, a person who deliberately chooses to be mediocre as a matter of principle. But life is not like that. There is no standing still in life, not when it comes to *ruchnius*.

Yaakov Avinu told us, "Behold, the ladder is standing on the ground and its top reaches into the heavens." The commentators see in these words that life is like a ladder. Either you go up, or you go down. You never remain stagnant.

Perhaps we can give this analogy a bit of a contemporary twist. Life is actually like an escalator. A down escalator. Our mission in life is to get to the top. If we walk up slowly, we will be carried down by the motion of the escalator. If we walk up quickly, we will stay in more or less the same place, since the down motion of the escalator and our own upward motion would cancel each other out. If, however, we make a tremendous effort to run up, we can overcome the downward motion and reach the top. That is what life is all about when it comes to matters of *ruchnius*. If you don't make an effort, the escalator will carry you down. There is no standing still in life.

The Midrash tells us that whenever an episode begins with the word *vayeishev*, and he sat, it is a sign of foreboding. Why is this so? The Maharal explains that sitting in one place invites calamity. Jews weren't made to sit still. A

Jew has to be constantly changing, constantly growing, constantly battling and struggling to reach new levels of achievement. Life is about change. Life is about growth. Life is about falling down and getting up and dusting yourself off and continuing the struggle. Life is an escalator.

The Midrash tells us that Hashem brought all the animals to Adam to be named. Adam looked at each one, discerned its essence and named it accordingly. Finally, Hashem asked Adam, "What name would you give to yourself? What should we call you?"

"I should be called Adam," he replied very wisely, "because I was taken from the earth [which is called *adamah*]."

Where exactly did the Midrash see Adam's great wisdom in this response? How does the connection between Adam and *adamah* reflect on the essence of the human being?

The Alter of Slobodka explains that an Adam, a human being, is indeed essentially like the *adamah*, the ground. You put things in the ground and they grow. You work, hoe, till, fertilize, prune, harvest and plant again. That's the nature of the ground. A human being is the same. His whole life is a continuous cycle of effort and growth, a constant battle that never ends.

Someone came to see Rav Yechezkel Abramsky and found him unusually happy and excited. He was beaming and smiling from ear to ear.

"Why is the *rav* so elated?" asked the visitor.

Rav Chatzkel shook his head and tried to brush the matter aside, but his visitor persisted. Finally, Rav Chatzkel relented.

"I'm embarrassed," he said, "but you know why I'm happy? A few minutes before you came in, I had an urge to take a candy into my mouth for no reason. I wasn't hungry. Just pure *yetzer hara*. And I resisted. I overcame the *yetzer hara*."

Here was a man in his 80s, the author of *Chazon*

Yechezkel, dayan on the London *beis din* and the Yerushalayim *beis din*. He could just sit back and relax while he looks back with satisfaction on a life well spent. Why is he so concerned about the *yetzer hara* and a piece of candy? Why? Because life never comes to a standstill. Even in his 80s, he is still struggling, still growing, still changing. The battle never comes to an end.

But our resistance to change goes deeper. It is not only because we don't want to disrupt our comfortable lives that we don't want to change. It is not only because we feel threatened and intimidated that we don't want to change. The truth is that Jewish people are almost genetically disinclined to change.

The Gemara (*Yevamos* 79a) describes Jewish people as bashful, compassionate and benevolent. But there is one more very distinctive Jewish characteristic. We are an *am keshei oref*, a stiff-necked, stubborn people that resists change. Sforno says that it is as though we have metal rods down our backs. We refuse to change, to listen, even to turn our necks.

After the Jewish people sinned with the Golden Calf, Hashem told Moshe Rabbeinu that He wanted to destroy them. What reason did He give? Not because they had committed so grievous a sin. Apparently, that alone would not have provoked such a harsh decree. Hashem was inclined to destroy them because "they are a stiff-necked people." They don't want to listen, they don't want to change.

How do you break that intransigence? How do you penetrate that wall?

Moshe Rabbeinu did do something to penetrate that wall. The Torah, at its very end, describes what he did as the most profound and unbelievable act of his life. Moshe Rabbeinu broke the *Luchos*, the Holy Tablets of the Ten Commandments. He needed desperately to get the attention of the Jewish nation. He needed to get the message through to them. Sometimes that takes drastic action. Sometimes that takes breaking the *Luchos*, the Tablets that had been inscribed by Hashem's own finger

Unfortunately, that is what it sometimes takes to get our attention. When tragedies happen in our midst, these too may be the *Luchos* breaking, so to speak. These too may sometimes be a message to get our attention. Stop being so stubborn, so set in your ways that you refuse to change.

Several years ago, a message was delivered to the Jewish community of Portland, Oregon, and it did indeed get their attention. Portland had not had an Orthodox *rav* for over 40 years. One Yom Kippur night, as they were taking out the *Sifrei Torah* for Kol Nidrei, one of the honorary bearers of a *Sefer Torah* collapsed, and the *Sefer Torah* fell to the ground. The people were shocked and disoriented. What could this mean?

One congregant offered an interpretation. "If the Torah falls on the ground," he declared, "that means that we're not supporting the Torah."

As a result of that incident, Portland today has an Orthodox *shul* and an Orthodox *rav*. The "breaking of their *Luchos*" got their attention. They got the message, and they changed.

There are so many messages in life. Hashem sends them all the time, but we have to listen. If we're stubborn and inflexible, the message can go right by us. If, however, we're sensitive and caring and open, we hear the message.

Let us consider two message recipients who are at the opposite ends of the spectrum, Bilaam and Rabbi Akiva.

Bilaam mounts his donkey and sets off on a mission to curse the Jewish people. The donkey refuses to budge. Bilaam strikes the donkey. Suddenly, the donkey starts to speak to him. Now, what would you do in such a situation? You don't have a donkey, but you probably have a car. Imagine then that one morning your car doesn't start. You get angry, and you bang on the steering wheel. Suddenly, your car starts talking back to you. Would you get into a conversation with your car? Or would you grab your head in fright and wonder what on earth is happening?

Well, Bilaam seems to take his donkey's transformation in stride. In fact, he actually gets into an argument with his donkey. Bilaam doesn't hear. He doesn't get the message. And when the whole episode is over, the Torah tells us that "Bilaam returned to his place." Everything went back to the way it was. There had not been even one iota of change. He didn't hear the message.

Contrast that with Rabbi Akiva who is intrigued by the sight of water dripping onto a stone. He comes to the conclusion that if water can make a stone smooth, the Torah certainly can have an effect on him. He observes a simple act of nature and changes his life. He doesn't even need any talking donkeys. Why? He hears the message.

Rav Yisrael Salanter once passed by a shoemaker's stall late at night and saw that the shoemaker was still there.

"Why are you still working?" he asked the shoemaker. "It's so late at night. Why don't you go home?"

"Because as long as there's oil in the lamp," said the shoemaker, "there's work to do."

What a stunning statement! thought Rav Yisrael Salanter. As long as there is oil in the lamp, as long as the *neshamah* burns within us, there's still work to do. Rav Yisrael Salanter heard the message delivered to him through the mouth of a simple shoemaker. Why? Because he was open to it. He was receptive. We all get messages, but some of us just let them go by unread.

Some time ago, I went to visit my mother in Seattle. That year, we had decided my mother was no longer up to making Pesach. Instead of us coming to her, this year she would come to us for Pesach.

In anticipation of my visit, my mother packed up her Pesach dishes so they could be shipped to Baltimore. I loaded them into the trunk and the back seat of the car, and we set off for the post office together.

On the way, I told her, "Do me a favor. When we get there, let me take in the boxes. Do not shlep the boxes yourself. It's not good for you."

Sure enough, as soon as we got there, she opened the rear door while I was opening the trunk. I saw she was intent on shlepping some of the boxes.

"Please don't take the boxes," I pleaded with her. "I'll shlep the boxes."

I went to the back seat to take out the boxes, and I saw my mother going to the trunk to get those boxes.

"Please, I'm begging you," I called out in frustration. "Don't take the boxes."

While this was going on, a man was standing nearby in the parking lot, watching with a wry smile on his face what was going on.

He gave me a wink, rolled his eyes and said, "Mothers!"

"Isn't that the truth," I responded.

"Well," he said, "be glad you still have one."

Now that's a message; no question about it. A message delivered by a man in a post office parking lot.

Messages can also come from an altogether different direction, even from our own mouths. Listen to this story.

A woman interested in becoming religious is studying in Yerushalayim. She is learning about Torah and *mitzvos*, making real progress. She is on the way.

One day, she announces to her teacher that she has decided to leave.

"Why are you leaving?" the teacher asks her.

"Because I'm pregnant," she says. "I want to terminate my pregnancy."

"But why do you want to terminate your pregnancy?" the teacher asks.

"Because I want to embark on a career," she says. "This pregnancy is just going to make things too difficult."

"What does your husband say?" he asks her.

"He stands by my decision."

The teacher sees that he is out of his depth. There is no way he will ever convince this woman not to have an abortion. So he tries a new approach.

"Listen," he says, "if you're going to have an abortion, you should be aware that it is a dangerous procedure. Let me take you to a great rabbi, a holy person. Let's ask him for a blessing to get you through this abortion safely. I'll go along to act as your interpreter."

The woman agrees, and the teacher takes her to Rav Shlomo Zalman Auerbach.

"I would like a blessing," she says to R' Shlomo Zalman. "You see, I'm going to terminate my pregnancy."

"Why would you want to terminate your pregnancy?" asks Rav Shlomo Zalman.

"Because I want to pursue a career," she says.

"What kind of career do you want to pursue?"

"I want to become a doctor."

"And why do you want to become a doctor?"

"Because a doctor saves lives."

Rav Shlomo Zalman smiles and asks, "Really? And what is so important about saving lives?"

The woman is startled by the question. She gives Rav Shlomo Zalman a strange look, as if she was wondering if he was senile. "What's important about saving lives?" she says. "Saving a life is the most important thing in this world."

All of a sudden the significance of what she has just said hits her. She looks at Rav Shlomo Zalman, then she points to her abdomen. "You don't mean this, do you?"

Rav Shlomo Zalman says, "It can become a life, a living human being."

The woman nods in acceptance. She has just heard a message, not from a donkey's mouth, not from water falling on a stone, not from a shoemaker, not from a man in a parking lot, but from her own mouth.

We have established that we are resistant to change for various reasons. We have established that it is a hard thing to do. We have established how important it is to be open to change. But there is one final, very critical point to be made about change. It is a wonderful experience.

People who can change feel exhilarated. They feel they are in control of their lives, that they make their decisions rather than having their decisions made for them. People who can change feel closer to Hashem. People who can change feel closer to each other.

And people most definitely can change. They do change.

Talk about change. Look at all the thousands of our Jewish brothers and sisters who have become *baalei teshuvah*. Many of these people have given up ties with family and friends, careers and livelihoods, all just to live by their convictions.

Talk about change. Look at the thousands and thousands of people who have undertaken strict observance of *shemiras halashon*. Just one generation ago, *shemiras halashon* was a *mitzvah* that was trampled in the dust. Today, we are seeing the results of a revolution. People speak differently, act differently, think differently.

Attitudes change. Perceptions change.

People change.

Of course, it's hard. The difficulties may sometimes seem insurmountable, but it can be done, and the reward is immense.

I once heard about a woman who was in charge of a major business in New York City and earning a high six-figure salary. She began to study and eventually decided to become observant. Finally, she invited her rabbi to her home to make her kitchen kosher. When the rabbi arrived, he saw a pack of Chiclets, a decidedly unkosher gum, lying on the coffee table.

"If you want to make your home kosher," the rabbi said, "the first thing you have to do is get rid of the Chiclets. They're not kosher."

"Give up my Chiclets?" said the woman. "That's it. I can't keep kosher."

Today, of course, this woman is married and living in Yerushalayim. But at the time, the Chiclets loomed large in her mind. How could she give them up? How could she make such a change?

We all have our Chiclets. We all have some reprehensible items we cling to so tightly that it seems as if our lives depend on them. But no matter what that something is, it can be done. We can give it up. We can change.

The key to change is starting small. If you say you're never going to speak *lashon hara* again, you're setting yourself up for failure. Instead, undertake not to speak *lashon hara* from 2 o'clock to 3 o'clock in the afternoon for the next month. That has a much better chance of working, and then you can go on from there. One step at a time, that's the key to successful change.

Take small steps, steps you can accomplish with a high likelihood of success. Prove to yourself that you can change, and you will find that it gets easier with every step you take.

Emus, Hondas and Cynicism

WHAT DO EMUS AND HONDAS HAVE TO DO WITH cynicism? That's a tough question, especially since most people don't know what emus are. All right, for those of you who don't know, emus are big ostrich-like birds. Recently, entrepreneurs in Texas have begun raising emus in the hope they would replace beef in the American diet of the 21st century. Emu meat is low in cholesterol, high in protein; it has all the advantages of beef with none of the disadvantages. This was such a promising industry that a pair of breeding emus sold for $45,000.

So what do these wonder birds have to do with cynicism? A lot.

At about the time that emu farming was gathering steam and credibility, Honda Motors was producing a commercial to promote its Accord automobile. In the commercial — which I happened to hear a report about on National Public Radio — a young man was faced with many career choices as he prepared to make his way in the world. But when it came to choosing an automobile, there really were no choices other than the Honda Accord.

To catch the attention of the public, the commercial mockingly portrayed one loser profession after another which the young man must consider and reject. Among the ridiculed professions was emu farming. Imagine, some people actually think emu meat will replace beef. Only hicks from Texas, the commercial implied, could have such a ridiculous idea.

The commercial was, of course, not intended as an attack on the fledgling emu-farming industry. Emu farmers were simply used as a foil for the sarcastic commentary that would catch the attention of prospective buyers and direct them towards the peerless Honda Accord. But believe it or not, this commercial destroyed the emu-farming industry. Within a short time, a pair of breeding emus was selling for $500, a decline of 90 percent from its earlier $45,000 price tag. The State of Texas brought suit against Honda Corporation of America, claiming that Honda had defamed the emus and the entire emu industry. The case is pending.

So what do these emus and Hondas tell us about cynicism? They show us how destructive even one little throwaway line of mockery can be. One line of *bittul*, as a put-down is called in Hebrew, can wipe out years of effort.

What is the significance of the word *bittul*? Think of it this way. Before Pesach, we have a process called *bittul chametz*, by which we verbally negate the *chametz* and render it non-existent. Even if it's there and you see it, for all intents and purposes, the *chametz* has been evaporated by your words. Words can also wreak havoc with people and their livelihoods. One cynical sneer can evaporate a lifetime of effort. Such is the malignant power wielded by cynics.

Cynicism, as defined by the dictionary, is the state of being scornful of the motives or the virtues of others, of mocking and sneering. That's a cynic: someone who knocks, mocks, denigrates and puts down. A cynic is a fault-finder, a person who always seeks and pinpoints the faults in people, in institutions, in ideas.

The Hebrew word for cynic is *letz*. A *letz* is not a funny guy, a stand-up comedian. That is an incorrect translation. A *letz* is a cynic, a mocker, an evaporator of people.

Unfortunately, there are numerous Jewish *letzim*. We all know them and meet them wherever we go. But why would a person want to be a *letz*? Why would a person want to tear down other people and destroy them? Why would a person want to cause hardship and pain to people who have done him no harm? Why does such a sinister thing exist in our circles? And what can we as a society and a people do about it? These are very troubling questions indeed.

It would be easy to say that our own Jewish community is really not cynical; that the cynicism we encounter is no more than the inevitable reflection of the cynicism which infects American society at large. But that is not the answer.

There is, of course, no denying that America suffers from rampant cynicism. A recent study of current journalism discovered over 5,000 mentions of the word cynics or cynicism in either the title or the first paragraph of over 5,000 articles — and all this in just one year. The libraries are full of books that explore and analyze the roots of this malaise of endemic cynicism. If cynicism is so rife in America, the argument goes, we cannot isolate ourselves totally, and therefore, it is to be expected that even Orthodox Jews will become cynical.

But this answer is too facile, too smug. It shies away from the reality of the contemporary Jewish scene. We need more fundamental answers and more courage to face them. Furthermore, have we ever stopped to think why indeed America has become such a nation of cynics? It might be instructive.

Let us listen to what Rav Yitzchak Hutner, the Rosh Yeshivah of Yeshivas Rabbeinu Chaim Berlin, has to say on the subject. Writing in his classic *Pachad Yitzchak*, Rav

Hutner contends that the struggle against cynicism forms the paradigm of the epic battle between the Jewish people and Amalek. Amalek's attack on the Jewish people was far more than a military confrontation between two nations. It was far more than just a battle of swords and chariots, of guns and tanks. The battle between the Jewish people and Amalek centered on the very issue of cynicism.

There is a powerful tendency in human nature, Rav Hutner writes, a veritable passion, to denigrate, to mock, to tear down, to eliminate others. There is a tendency to take that which is noble and important and holy and to find within it the little hairline crack which can be used to bring the entire edifice tumbling down. It is a particularly virulent form of the *yetzer hara*. People have a *yetzer hara* for money, for honor, for carnal pleasures. People have a *yetzer hara* for all sorts of forbidden things. And they also have a *yetzer hara* to destroy other people, to be cynical, to put people down, to ridicule all that is important and holy.

The nation of Amalek personifies this tendency. When the Jewish people came forth from Egypt, the world stood in awe of them and of the Almighty who had performed all the spectacular miracles on their behalf. The Jewish nation was important, revered. But Amalek could not tolerate it. And so they attacked to dispel the aura of Jewish invincibility, to show that the Jewish people were mere mortals after all, that they need not be held in awe and reverence. That was Amalek's motivation for the attack. It was not territorial. It was not political. It was not even ideological. It was cynical.

How do we understand this *yetzer hara*? We can understand why people would want money. We can understand why people would want honor. We can understand why people would want carnal pleasures. But why would people want to destroy others? Why would people want to tear down whatever is good, holy, important, serious and worthwhile in this world?

Perhaps it is because cynicism liberates. Perhaps it is because cynicism emancipates. If there is nothing worthy and important in this world, we are all free to do as we please. If there are no higher standards, we can all go wherever our fancy and our impulses take us. If the citadels of holiness can be ripped down, we are all released from personal responsibility.

That is what Amalek is all about. As Rav Hutner puts it in his inimitable fashion, Amalek represents the *koach hachillul*; but there is also an opposite tendency in human nature, which Rav Hutner calls the *koach hahillul*.

The battle lines are drawn: the *koach hachillul* versus the *koach hahillul*; the forces of sacrilege against the forces of reverence; Amalek against Yisrael. This is the battle, the struggle for the soul of the world. And Hashem tells the Jewish people to eradicate all traces of Amalek. Wipe them out. Eradicate them. They are your mortal enemy in this life-and-death struggle — not merely your physical mortal enemy but your spiritual mortal enemy. They despise all that you stand for, all that is holy, pure, fine and worthwhile in this world. They are the antithesis of the Jew.

There is a little bit of Amalek in each of us, Rav Hutner concludes, and that is why we have an inclination to be cynical, to mock and destroy.

So that is the philosophical basis of why people tend to be cynics. There is also a very real psychological basis.

Arrogance and egotism, for instance, can easily engender a desire to put down people and the institutions they represent. After all, who do they think they are? They are not religious enough, learned enough, smart enough, rich enough nor successful enough to expect a place in the sun. And so the arrogant, the *baal gaavah*, the sanctimonious will seek to put them in their place, and what more effective way is there than a good dose of cynicism?

Even more common, I suspect, than an overinflated ego as a cause of cynicism is an underinflated ego. People with low self-esteem feel threatened by other people and are therefore inclined to ridicule them and bring them down to their own level with a shot of cynicism.

Let's not forget jealousy as a motive for cynicism. How do jealous people deal with those who enjoy more blessings than they do? With cynical put-downs, of course.

We have a very potent mix here. We start with a little dash of Amalek in each of us that impels us to tear down whatever is important and holy. We stir in a little arrogance or low self-esteem, top it off with a dash of jealousy, and presto, what have we got? A cynic — a person who will capitalize on every opportunity and try to make snide comments about anything and anyone that might inspire admiration and respect! This is the genesis of a cynic.

But why today? These human tendencies and emotions have existed since time immemorial. Why then are we experiencing such an upsurge of cynicism? Going back 50 years, you will most certainly not find so many books and articles about cynicism. What has changed in the second half of the 20th century? What's different about our times?

It appears to me, therefore, that there is another ingredient to the witch's brew that produces cynicism. Cynicism is the child of disillusionment and disappointment. People become cynical when they lose faith and confidence in people and institutions. When they are let down too many times, they become determined never to trust again.

This gives us a little insight into the prevalence of cynicism in American society in the second half of this century. It has been a time of disappointments, large and small.

A famous syndicated columnist named Richard Reeves once wrote, "I've never really been the same since the double betrayals of the 1950s. Eisenhower lied to me and the rest of the world about the U-2 incident, and Walter O'Malley moved the Brooklyn Dodgers to Los Angeles."

Do you hear what turned Richard Reeves into a cynic? He had believed the president of the United States when he went on national television and said there had been no spy-plane overflights of Russia. But when the Russians produced Gary Powers, the downed American pilot, the president had to admit his lie. Presidents are not supposed to lie. That was number one. Number two was the betrayal by the owner of the Brooklyn Dodgers. Mr. Reeves had invested so much faith, passion and loyalty into his beloved Dodgers only to wake up one morning to discover that his team was moving to a city 3,000 miles away. And so, Mr. Reeves, child of the Fifties, was disappointed and became a cynic.

Those who came of age in the Sixties were disappointed by Vietnam and Kent State. In the Seventies, Watergate delivered disappointment in large measure. A president was convicted of high crimes and misdemeanors, a president who used his power to subvert the institutions of this government. In the Eighties, the Iran Contra affair disappointed people. And if you're just coming of age in the Nineties, the office of the presidency has become a laughingstock. Americans used to tell their children, "If you work hard, you can become president of the United States." Who would want to suggest that to their children today?

People have become turned off — turned off by their government, by their leaders, by their military, by all the institutions in which they had placed their faith. No wonder they have become cynical.

People are disappointed in Corporate America. They feel let down by major corporations which feel no compunction in downsizing and laying off people who have been with them for decades. They feel let down by American products which are shoddy and unreliable.

So if you can't trust the government, if you can't trust the military, if you can't trust the politicians, if you can't trust the corporations, whom can you trust? And if you cannot trust anyone, you become a cynic.

But why us? Why do Orthodox Jews become cynical? We should know better, shouldn't we?

King David writes in the very first chapter of *Tehillim*, "These are the fortunes of a man, that he did not walk by the guidance of villains, that he did not stop along the way of sinners, that he did not sit in the councils of mockers." Don't be a *letz*, a mocker, a cynic. So why do we do it?

The Gemara tells us, "Four groups of people will not be welcomed into the presence of the Almighty. Who are they? People who speak *lashon hara*; people who lie; people who curry favor through flattery; people who are cynical."

We have national campaigns against *lashon hara*. Everyone is learning about *shemiras halashon*, and the amount of *lashon hara* has really been drastically reduced. All because it is forbidden by the Torah. Well, cynicism is also forbidden. And yet, paradoxically, the more religious people become, the more they are inclined to view others with cynical eyes. So why do we do it?

Let me present a theory. Apparently, our Sages themselves have instructed us to be cynics. They have told us, "All mockery is forbidden except for mockery of idol worship." Never be a cynic, but when it comes to idolatry, be as cynical as you can be. Make fun of them. Mock them. Ridicule them. Why is this so? Why jeopardize this taboo by making an exception?

Rav Eliyahu Dessler explains that our Sages did this in response to a real need of the Jewish people. Two thousand years ago, we were the only monotheistic religion in a vast pagan sea. How could the Sages prevent the people from giving in to the pressure of their neighbors and succumbing to the predominant idol worship? How could we survive as a pure people? By allowing and encouraging the people to mock and ridicule idolatry.

Let's go back much further into the past, and once again, we find cynicism against idolatry. The scene is the top of Mount Carmel, and a dramatic contest is in progress.

Eliyahu, the Prophet Elijah, is on the one side and the priests of Baal are on the other. The challenge is to see who can bring down fire from the sky. The priests of the Baal bang their heads together but all to no avail. There is no fire forthcoming from the sky. And while this is going on, Eliyahu mocks them, "You know, maybe your god is sleeping. Maybe he is indisposed." Eliyahu is playing the role of *letz*! He is making a mockery of them. Obviously, mockery is fine when it comes to idolatry. You can make as much fun as you like, because that is the only way to survive.

Today we don't have the old forms of idolatry. People don't genuflect to little stone or wood figurines. But there are other idols out there, cultural icons that exert a powerful attraction on us. So what are we going to do? How can we protect ourselves? We have to revert to mockery. We ridicule these attractions so that we should not succumb to their lure. We have no choice. This is what we have to do. This is what our Sages want us to do.

But herein lies the rub. We can lock *lashon hara* away in a forbidden zone, because we are *never* allowed to speak *lashon hara*. We can lock dishonesty away in a forbidden zone, because we are never allowed to lie. We can lock sycophantic flattery away in a forbidden zone, because it is always forbidden. but we cannot do the same for cynicism. We cannot say, "Never be a cynic." It is simply not true. From time to time, you have to be a cynic. Once you've let the genie out of the bottle, though, it's hard to push him back in.

That, I believe, is why Orthodox Jews have become such terrible cynics. We are so accustomed to using cynicism to protect ourselves against the dominant culture that we sometimes have difficulty controlling it.

So how indeed can we control it? How on earth are we supposed to stop ourselves from falling into this trap of unwarranted cynicism?

Number one, we have to come out and say that cynicism is not acceptable. We have to tell our children, our families, our students, our congregants that cynicism is a terrible, terrible trait. Have you ever met a person who boasted about speaking *lashon hara*? Of course not. Some people do it, but they are not proud of it. But you have probably heard religious people pride themselves on being cynical. I certainly have, and more than once. "You know what? I'm a big cynic." We have to stop that by attaching a stigma to cynicism, just as we have attached a stigma to *lashon hara*.

We have to come to the realization that cynicism is bad, that it's destructive, that it's pernicious and that it destroys. We have to come to the realization that uncontrolled habitual cynicism leads people to the belief that nothing in this world is worth anything, that cynicism is a slippery slope that will plunge you into the abyss. No one should even have the temerity to pride himself on being a big cynic, as though it were a badge of honor.

Let us check out some cynics in history. Esau, Jacob's brother, was a cynic. On the day his illustrious grandfather Abraham dies, what does this fellow go out and do? He goes hunting and comes back famished. His brother Jacob offers him a bowl of lentil soup in return for the firstborn rights to the spiritual heritage of the Patriarchs. Esau consents without any argument. "Fine," he says. "Give me a bowl of soup and the firstborn rights are yours." The Torah concludes, "And Esau made a mockery of the birthright." He thumbed his nose at the birthright, at the memory of his sainted grandfather, at everything holy. He was the classic cynic, denigrating anything and everything. He considered nothing sacred.

Esau's descendant was the hotheaded Amalek who could not endure the spectacle of all the world standing in awe of the triumphant Jewish people.

Amalek's descendant was Haman, who followed in the footsteps of his infamous forebears. The Baal HaTurim points out that the word *vayivez*, and he mocked, appears only twice in all of the Torah: once with regard to Esau, who made a mockery of the birthright, and then with regard to Haman. The Midrash considers Haman a mocker the son of a mocker, a cynic the son of a cynic. Nothing is important. Nothing is sacred. If a nation gets in your way, just wipe them out. What does it matter anyway? Nothing matters.

That is the path of cynicism. Nothing moves a cynic. Nothing disturbs him. Nothing inspires him.

How often does it happen that a rabbi makes an impassioned speech about an issue of vital importance to the community and one clown sitting in the back makes a wisecrack that wipes everything out? With one little remark, one mere twist of the nose, that single clown can counteract all the rabbi's efforts. The cynic is immune to inspiration, and he will make sure no one else is inspired either. Is that a life?

Eliyahu Hanavi apparently was also worried about the clown sitting in the back. When he confronted the priests of the Baal on Mount Carmel, he claimed that he alone could bring down fire from heaven. "Answer me, Hashem," he cried out. "O answer me." What were these two pleas? Our Sages tells us (Berachos 6b) that the first plea was for the miracle itself, that fire should descend from the heavens. The second plea was that people should not say he had done it through witchcraft.

At this transcendent moment, the crowning glory of his career, when he is about to sanctify the Name of Heaven before a vast multitude, Eliyahu is worried about the boys in the back who will snigger and snicker and whisper to each other that it was no big deal. Anyone with an updated witchcraft manual could pull it off. Yes, Eliyahu is worried about the cynics, and he prays for protection against them.

The bottom line is: How can we convince people not to be cynical? To be perfectly realistic, it just may not be enough to simply rant and rave about the evils of cynicism and the unholy heritage of Esau, Amalek and Haman. For some people, all this is too abstract, too much philosophy. They need some practical motivation. Very well then; let's give them practical motivation in the form of three very clear choices.

Choice number one. Would you rather be happy or cynical?

Almost invariably, cynicism and happiness occur in inverse proportions. The greater the cynicism, the smaller the happiness. The Psalmist tells us (97:11), "*Ohr zarua latzaddik uleyishrei leiv simchah.* A light has been planted for the righteous, and happiness for the straight-hearted." *Yishrei leiv*, straight-hearted people, enjoy the blessing of happiness. How do we define *yishrei leiv*? Who are considered straight-hearted people?

Rav Hutner points out that Targum translates *uleyishrei leiv* as *uleteritzi liba*. Straight-hearted people are those whose hearts are full of *terutzim*, people who are inclined to explain away everything that may appear negative. They are explainers, not complainers, the exact opposite of cynics. These are the people for whom life holds happiness in store.

There is a perfect logic to this. Life, under the best of circumstances, is full of disappointments, and our level of happiness is determined by how we deal with those disappointments. If we explain them away, we can be happy. But if we complain, we are doomed to misery.

Furthermore, all people will most likely disappoint us at one time or another. Complainers harp on the mistakes of their friends and lose the friendships in the process; they are left to stew alone in their cynicism. This is not exactly a formula for happiness. Explainers, on the other hand, see the good in all people, and consequently, they maintain very wide circles of friends; everyone wants to be their friend.

The Mishnah in *Avos* (1:6) tells us, "Provide yourself with a mentor, acquire for yourself a friend, and judge all people favorably." What is the connection between the first part of the statement and the second? What does judging people favorably have to do with mentors and friends?

It's really very simple.

If you want to have a long and solid relationship with your mentor, your *rebbe*, judge him favorably. Give him the benefit of the doubt. If he seems to have done something wrong, explain it away.

If you want to keep your relationships with your friends, judge them favorably. If they didn't come to the *simchah* or the *shivah* or whatever, give them the benefit of the doubt. Explain it to yourself. If you really want to, you will undoubtedly be able to come up with some decent explanations.

Explainers keep relationships. Complainers don't. Explainers are enriched by other people. Complainers aren't.

Choice number two. Do you want to be wise or foolish?

According to King Solomon in *Mishlei* (14:9), "Fools find fault, but among the sincere there is forgiveness." This is the acid test. If you find fault, you are a fool. Rabbeinu Yonah explains that it is the nature of fools to seek out the negative sides of people and never to give praise. Why are they fools? Because if they always criticize, always put people down, they will never enjoy life.

The Midrash describes the Jewish people at the shores of the sea with the Egyptians in hot pursuit. Hashem works an incredible miracle, and the sea splits open, leaving a pathway for them. So what do some of the people say? The Midrash tells us that they complain that there is mud on their shoes. Can you imagine? Mud on their shoes! Fools find fault. Hashem can tear open the sea for them, but they are dissatisfied because of the mud on their brand-new shoes.

Rabbeinu Yonah concludes with a powerful parable. A fool and a wise man walking on a road came across a rotting, putrid carcass.

"What an awful stink!" said the fool.

"Look how white its teeth are," the wise man countered.

Fools find fault. The wise find merit.

There is a famous story about Rav Eliezer Silver, one of the *gedolim* of the last generation, one of the founders of Agudath Israel of America. Rav Silver, a member of Rav Chaim Ozer Grodzensky's rabbinical court in Vilna in the early part of the century, was widely known for his encyclopedic knowledge. He emigrated to America and served as rabbi in Harrisburg, Pennsylvania, and afterwards in Cincinnati, Ohio.

After the Second World War, Rav Silver was extremely active in bringing Holocaust survivors out from Europe and in retrieving Jewish children who had been given refuge in Christian homes during the Holocaust.

On one of his visits to a displaced persons camp, he met a man who had suffered in the camps for years.

"I will never again pray in my life," said the man. "I will never pick up a *siddur* as long as I live."

Rav Silver studied the man. "Really?" he said. "And why not?"

"Because there was a Jew in the camp who had a *siddur*. So did he let others pray in it? Not unless they paid him. Half a day's rations, that was his price. Anyone who wanted to pray in the *siddur* had to give him half a day's rations. What an outrage! This man is running a brisk business taking rations from starving men. So I decided that if this is what religious Jews are like, I want no part of it."

Rav Silver smiled and shook his head. "I don't understand you," he said. "Why do you look at the man who rented out his *siddur*? Why don't you look at all those people who gave up their precious rations for the privilege of holding a *siddur* in their hands for a few minutes? This is what Jews are like, and you should be proud to be one of us."

Fools find fault, but the wise find merit.

Choice number three. What kind of children do you want to have?

There are no shortcuts to raising good children, no magic formulas. But one thing is indisputable. Children learn from their parents. If children see a positive, upbeat, trusting attitude in their parents, they will seek to develop a similar attitude themselves.

Do you want your children to be kind-hearted, caring,

enthusiastic people and go through life with a positive out-look? Show them that you yourself are an explainer, that you always see the good in people.

Do you want your children to be masters of the one-liner? Do you want them to be hardened cynics at age 10? Do you want them to sneer at their teachers and their peers? You can accomplish this, too. Just show them that you are a cynic, that you want to tear down everything others build up.

But I'll let you in on a little secret. I don't think there is anyone in the world who wants his children to be cynical. It's a privilege some people reserve for themselves alone.

In the Mishkan, the voice of Hashem emanated from between the two cherubs that sat astride the *aron hakodesh*, the holy ark. Why? I once heard an explanation from Rav Shmuel Rozovsky. You can have the holiest spot on earth and the holiest voice in the universe, but if the people receiving it do not have the childlike enthusiasm for learning, it won't penetrate.

We need to ensure that our children do not lose the enthusiasm that comes so naturally to them. Cynicism can stifle it. Mockery can smother it. If all they hear at our tables is cynicism, sharp one-liners, negativity and derision, don't expect them to be enthusiastic little angels.

Our parents had a much harder life than we do. Some of them barely survived Europe, some lived through the Depression. They didn't have much money, and yet they gave us a positive outlook on life. Yet many of us who have so much, whose lives are so much more secure, so much more affluent, are clambering up the slippery slope of cynicism.

I wonder why. I wonder if it is because our parents were happy just to be alive, to have roofs over their heads and shirts on their backs. In the long run, there is no greater antidote to cynicism than being intensely thankful for what you have.

The Gemara says in Berachos (60b), "A person should always be accustomed to saying that all Hashem does is for the best." Why does the Gemara express this thought in such a cumbersome way? It would have been simpler to say, "A person should say that all Hashem does is for the best." Or even shorter, "All Hashem does is for the best."

A friend of mine, Rabbi Yaakov Luban, offered a brilliant insight. One of the most difficult things in the world, if not the most difficult, is to say with true conviction that all Hashem does is for the best. And guess what? If the first time in his life a person says those words is when he is faced with tragedy, it will be nothing but lip service.

The conviction that all Hashem does is for the best must be built up over a long time. If your toast falls to the floor buttered-side down, say with feeling, "*Gam zu letovah*. This is also for the best." You will find that acceptable. It will enter your brain and your heart without overloading your circuits.

Then when you get stuck in traffic and miss your plane, which is somewhat tougher than buttered toast falling on the floor, you will find it easier to say, "*Gam zu letovah*. This is also for the best." The words will sink deeper into your brain and your heart, and your conviction will grow.

And then if something serious should ever happen, Heaven forbid, you will really be equipped to put real conviction into saying, "*Gam zu letovah*. This is also for the best."

People need to condition themselves; they have to become accustomed to saying that all Hashem does is for the best. You can't just get up and say it. You have to train yourself to believe it deep down inside your heart. You have to become accustomed to it. You have to make it a habit.

This, I believe, is also the key to overcoming cynicism. We have to develop the habit of being positive instead of negative, of seeing the good instead of the bad. We have to raise our consciousness. We have to be on the lookout for — and squelch — those almost involuntary little cynical remarks that escape from our mouths. Then little by little, we will form the habits of looking at the world in a positive light. And we will be immeasurably enriched, both by the increased happiness in our own lives and by the profound joy of seeing our children blossom into the kindhearted and enthusistic people we want them to be.

Your Neighbor's Donkey

MOST PEOPLE DON'T REALIZE HOW GREAT AND sinister a role envy plays in our lives. But stop and think about it. Don't we all deal with envy practically every single day? We would have no problem driving the car we have, but when we look across the street and see what our neighbor is driving, our car suddenly loses its luster. We would have no problem staying home in the summer or going on a modest vacation, but when we hear where our neighbor is going, we feel impelled to revise our travel plans.

Our children come to us when they're little, and they say, "But he got a new bike! I want a new bike, too!"

They get a little older and the requests get a little larger, and the problems of dealing with envy become more severe.

What happens in January when schools have intersession?

All along the East Coast, hundreds of teenagers head for the warm climes of Florida and points further south and west. So what do you do when your children come to you and say that everyone else is going, so why can't they? And maybe you cannot afford the cost of a midwinter Florida vacation for your children, or maybe you simply don't want to be part of that culture. So how do you deal with the pressure generated by envy?

And speaking of January, this is the month in which Bais Yaakov girls receive responses to their applications to the various seminaries in Israel. For those unfamiliar with this situation, let me tell you that the competition is fierce. My wife used to teach 12th grade in the Bais Yaakov of Baltimore. She would dread that awful week in January when the replies would come back from the seminaries, when the verdicts would come down, declaring who was accepted and who was rejected. My wife didn't even have to ask. Just one look at their reddened eyes and tear-streaked faces and she knew the entire story.

So your daughter may ask you, "Why wasn't I accepted? Why did they want her but not me?" What do you say?

Or sometimes your son may see his friends getting engaged while things are not going so smoothly for him. "Why could he find his *basherte*," he wants to know, "while I'm just sitting here?" What do you say?

And believe me, when you listen to them, you can hear it clearly. A major part of the problem is that they do not have what others are getting. If the entire class had been rejected by the seminaries, if the entire group had not yet found mates, it would not be nearly as disturbing.

So this terrible problem of envy affects us as little children. It affects us as adolescents. It affects us as young adults. It affects us as mature adults. It affects us from cradle to grave.

How can we deal with it? How can we avoid being envious and jealous of our peers and friends?

The problem of jealousy is an important and recurring

theme in the Torah. The story of Kayin and Hevel. is about jealousy. The story of Yosef and his brothers is about jealousy. The story of Shaul Hamelech and David Hamelech is about jealousy. Why does the Torah devote so much ink to the pitfalls of jealousy? Because human beings have to deal with jealousy day in day out, year after year, for all of their entire lives.

Let us return for a moment to the tragic incident of Kayin and Hevel. Both brought sacrifices. Hevel's was accepted, but Kayin's was not.

Kayin was the first person in the history of the world who had to compete, the first person in the history of the world who came in second. He was the first person in the history of the world who had to deal with jealousy. He was so consumed with jealousy that he actually killed his brother. And thus he became the first person in the history of the world to commit murder, the first to commit fratricide.

So what does this story tell us?

A lot.

First, it tells us that jealousy is triggered not so much by objects as by people. We are not actually jealous of what they have but of their having it. It's not the thing itself that matters, but that they have it and we don't. Kayin did not fly into a murderous rage because his sacrifice was rejected. No, that wouldn't have been so terrible. It was that Hevel's sacrifice was accepted while his wasn't. That was more than he could bear.

When my children were very young, I took them to a restaurant. We sat down at the table, and there was a container of toothpicks in the center of the table. The toothpicks were totally ignored as we discussed the menu. But then one of my children decided to take a toothpick, and suddenly the other children were all clamoring for toothpicks. Now trust me on this; 6-year-olds and 8-year-olds don't need toothpicks. So why did they want toothpicks all of a sudden? Because the others had toothpicks and they didn't.

Let me tell you a story about Rav Chaim Soloveitchik, the famous *rav* of Brisk. The chief judge of Rav Chaim's *beis din*, his rabbinical court, was a great scholar named Rav Simchah Zelig.

It once happened that a butcher came into the *beis din* with a question regarding an animal he had just slaughtered. He had found a lesion on one of its internal organs and he wanted to know whether or not the animal was kosher.

Rav Simchah Zelig looked at the evidence and then considered the question very carefully. In those days, there were no real options for disposing of non-kosher animals. Thus, declaring an animal non-kosher was no simple matter — it involved very great financial loss, very many rubles. Unfortunately, however, Rav Simchah Zelig could not find any basis for declaring the animal kosher.

"I'm sorry," he said. "This animal is not kosher. It can't be used."

The man sighed as he heard the ruling. He nodded in acceptance and walked out without a whimper.

Three months later, the same man appeared before Rav Simchah Zelig once again, this time to litigate a dispute between him and another person. The disputed amount was a paltry 75 rubles. Rav Simchah Zelig ruled against the man, and it cost him 75 rubles.

The man exploded in anger, shouting at Rav Simchah Zelig and cursing him. The screams were so loud that Rav Chaim heard him and came running. Afraid the man would become violent, Rav Chaim ordered him to leave.

"I don't understand," said Rav Simchah Zelig when he was finally alone with Rav Chaim. "Three months ago this man comes into my court. I rule against him and it costs him 1500 rubles, but he doesn't say a thing. Today he comes into my court, he loses 75 rubles, and he goes wild. It doesn't make any sense."

"The money has nothing to do with it," Rav Chaim replied. "It's all about winning and losing. In the case of the animal, there were no winners and losers, just a question about a piece of meat that had to be resolved. But today was a different story altogether. Today he lost and someone else won. That was unacceptable."

It's not the money. It's not the toothpicks. It's being second when someone else is first. It's not having when someone else does have.

Let us now get back to the story of Kayin and Hevel. Let us listen to the advice Hashem offers Kayin on dealing with envy.

"Why are you upset?" Hashem tells Kayin. "If you improve you will surely be uplifted. But if you don't improve, sin lurks in the doorway."

Why are you so upset, Kayin? Why are you letting your feelings of envy and jealousy overcome you? Learn from what happened. Improve. Harness your envy and channel it into positive things. Grow from this experience. If you use it to improve yourself, you will be uplifted. But remember, if you don't improve, if you stew in your jealousy, if you don't deal with your envy, sin crouches in the doorway. You will be plagued and destroyed by your jealousy and envy. They will haunt you until your dying day.

That's the lesson of jealousy. We have to learn how to deal with it, and we have to teach our children how to deal with it. When we feel an attack of envy coming on, we have to face it head on and grow from it. Then we will be uplifted. Otherwise, we will be smothered by it for the rest of our lives.

I once heard a story about a gravely ill man lying immobilized and connected to tubes and monitors in an intensive care unit. His prospects for recovery were questionable at best, and the man was despondent. Who can blame him? It was a terrible situation. He was constantly morose and withdrawn, barely acknowledging family and friends who came to visit him.

One day, a close friend, who was among his frequent visitors, walked in fully expecting another 15 minutes of gloom and doom. But to his surprise, the patient was chipper and cheerful. His wife was sitting in a chair nearby, reading a book.

"Well, I'm glad to see you in good spirits, my friend," he said. "You must have heard some good news."

"Y-yes, I s-sure did," said the patient with great effort.

"How wonderful!" said the friend. "Tell me about it. What happened? Have they found a new medication for you? Have your tests shown great improvement? Tell me."

The patient shook his head. He tried to speak, but he could not get the words out. Instead, he motioned to his wife to relate the good news that had so cheered him up.

"You know that manufacturer from Detroit who undercut my husband's business 35 years ago?" she asked.

"Yes," said the friend. "The man your husband blames for his problems."

"That's right, that's the guy," said the patient's wife. "Well, today the newspapers reported that the guy was killed in a car crash."

Incredible, isn't it? Here's a man hooked up to life-support systems, breathing through tubes in his nose and being fed through tubes in his veins, and what makes him happy? What puts him in a good mood? That he is alive and his enemy is dead.

Sin lurks in the doorway. It can affect us and haunt us and pervert us until our dying day.

The Midrash Shmuel on *Avos* presents a very illuminating parable about two people of different natures. One was an extremely envious person, the other an insatiable pleasure seeker. Satan comes to them and says, "Gentlemen, I'll make you a deal. I'll give one of you whatever you want. Make a wish — whatever you want — and it's yours. Just one condition. Whatever you get, your friend is going to get twice as much."

Both people faced a terrible dilemma.

The envious person could not deal with someone else getting twice as much as he did. "Whatever I'm going to wish for," he thought, "the other guy is going to get twice as much. I can't live with it."

The pleasure-seeker could not deal with it either. "How can I stand the sight of so much pleasure," he thought, "and not be able to enjoy it?"

So they went back and forth, each one pushing the choice onto the other. You choose. No, you choose. No, you choose.

Reluctantly, the envious person agreed to choose first. "What should I ask for?" he thought furiously. "Should I ask for a million dollars? I can't, because then he'll get two million. Should I ask for a 25-room mansion? I can't, because then he'll get a 50-room palace. So what should I do?"

Finally, the envious person came to his decision. He turned to Satan and said, "Okay, I made up my mind. I want you to take out one of my eyes."

This, points out the Midrash Shmuel, is how twisted and warped we can become. This is what envy can accomplish. A person who is ruled by envy would forgo the fondest wishes of his heart and ask to have his eye put out, just as long as someone else does not have more than he does. It is absolutely mindboggling.

Envy destroys, warps, corrodes, corrupts, perverts.

Moreover, not only is it destructive to be envious, it is also destructive to arouse envy in others.

Two of the scariest words in the Jewish language are *ayin hara*, the evil eye. People are afraid of *ayin hara*. How's your baby? Fine, pooh, pooh, pooh. The concept of *ayin hara*, the evil eye, is the great equalizer of the Jewish people. *Chasidim* are afraid of *ayin hara*. *Misnagdim* are afraid of *ayin hara*. *Ashkenazim* are afraid of *ayin hara*, *Sephardim* are afraid of *ayin hara*. Religious Jews are afraid of *ayin hara*. Secular Jews are afraid of *ayin hara*. Everyone is afraid of *ayin hara*.

I once heard that a baseball player on the New York Yankees was asked by a sports reporter from the *New York Times*, "To what do you attribute the improvement in your performance this year?"

So this ballplayer, who is a total Italian gentile, sticks out his arm to show off the *roite bendel* he's wearing around his wrist. For anyone who is not familiar with the *roite bendel*, it is a little red string bracelet which supposedly wards off the *ayin hara*. "I don't know for sure," he says, "but my grandmother from Sicily, she sent me this little red thing, and I wear it all the time, and I'm doing much better."

Apparently Sicilians worried about *ayin hara*, too.

I once saw a license plate on a very expensive automobile which read K9HARA. K Nine Hara, or rather, Kain Ayin Hara, which in Yiddish means, let there be no evil eye. I kid you not.

This *ayin hara* business, by the way, is not superstitious nonsense. According to the Gemara, it is one of the most lethal forces in the world. So how does it work? Can someone looking at me the wrong way affect me? Can someone giving me the evil eye cause injury to me? Even if I'm innocent? Even if I haven't done anything wrong? Even if I'm minding my own business?

Rav Eliahu Dessler, in his classic *Michtav M'Eliahu*, suggests that *ayin hara* cannot affect a person who is guiltless. *Ayin hara* can only affect a person who arouses envy in other people. In America we are told, "If you have it, flaunt it!" But the Torah begs to differ. If we have it and flaunt it, thereby causing envy in others, we are most definitely doing something wrong. And if we do arouse envy, the consequence is that we become vulnerable to the evil eye.

So what is the antidote? asks Rav Dessler. How can we protect ourselves if we are fortunate enough to have a wonderful home, wonderful children, a wonderful wife, a wonderful salary, a wonderful job? The only way, he explains, is to become a giver to the community rather than a taker. People look kindly on givers. They are inclined to be generous with people who give generously of their time, their money and their energies. But those who hoard it and flaunt it, who are miserly with the gifts Hashem has granted them, are not as pure as the driven snow. People are not inclined to cut them any slack, and thus, they become vulnerable to *ayin hara*.

So we see clearly that being envious can destroy us and causing others to be envious of us can also destroy us. So what do we do? How do contend with this overwhelming human tendency that ensnared such great people as Kayin, Yosef's brothers and Shaul Hamelech? What's the key?

The Gemara (*Shabbos* 152b) discusses the verse (*Mishlei* 14:30), "*Urekav atzamos kin'ah.* Jealousy rots the bones" What does this mean? The Gemara explains, "If a person is jealous in this world, his bones will decompose after he dies. But if he is not jealous in this world, his bones will remain intact after his death." In effect, one of the punishments for being jealous is post-mortem decomposition.

We know that Hashem punishes *midah keneged midah*, measure for measure. Therefore, there must be some connection between decomposition of the bones and being jealous. What is that connection?

The connection, I believe, goes to the very root of jealousy. A person who is jealous is fundamentally unhappy with who he is. He would much rather be someone else. He is unhappy with his wife. He is unhappy with his family. He is unhappy with his job. He is unhappy with his position. He wants to be someone else. He rejects who he is, his *atzmius*, his very essence. Therefore, he loses his *atzamos*, his bones, to decomposition.

It is no coincidence that the Hebrew words for essence and bones are so closely related. If there is any part of the human body that symbolizes what the person is, it is his bones. When a person "feels something in his bones," it penetrates to his very essence. Therefore, when a person is jealous and denies his essence, he causes the decomposition of his bones.

So how do we become happy with ourselves? How can a person come to the realization that he is unique and that there's no point in being someone else? How can a person come to the realization that he is not lacking anything he needs to be himself?

There is only one answer to these questions. It is a rock-solid, fundamental belief in the Creator of the Universe. A person must have a profound conviction that the Creator formed him and placed him here on this earth for his own special role and that He has given him *all the tools and the means he needs to fulfill that role.* Faith is the key to overcoming jealousy.

In *Mesilas Yesharim* (Ch.11), R' Moshe Chaim Luzatto writes that if people trusted in the hidden wisdom of Hashem they would have absolutely no reason to be jealous of what others possess. If a person truly believed that there is a Creator Who controls this world and sends people down to fulfill a unique purpose; if a person truly believed that the Creator watches over our every step and provides us with the ability to do what He wants us to do, how could he be jealous of someone else?

The Rikanti writes that the *mitzvah* of *lo sachmod,* do not covet, is fundamental to all the *mitzvos* in the Torah. Let us stop and think about this for a moment.

The *Aseres Hadibros,* the Ten Commandments, are the fundamentals of Judaism. Every single one of them is a fundamental of the faith. So let us begin.

Anochi Hashem Elokecha. I am Hashem, your Lord. Faith in the Almighty is the basis of our religion.

Lo yihyeh lecha elohim acherim. You shall not have other gods. Of course. Idol worship is out. There cannot be two Gods.

Lo sisa. Don't mention Hashem's Name in vain. Reverence is critical.

Zachor es yom Hashabbos lekadsho. By observing and sanctifying Shabbos, we bear witness that Hashem created the world in six days. Very important.

Kabed es avicha ve'es imecha. Honoring parents conditions us to be grateful to the source of our benefits, feelings ultimately channeled into our relationship with Hashem.

Lo sirtzach. Murder. *Lo sinaf.* Adultery. *Lo signov.* Kidnapping. *Lo sa'aneh berei'acha eid sheker.* Bearing false witness. All these are antithetical to faith in a benevolent Creator Who seeks a just and moral social order. These are, therefore, important fundamentals of Judaism.

Lo sachmod aishes rei'echa . . . vechamoro vechol asher lerei'echa. Jealousy. Don't covet your neighbor's wife or his donkey or any of his possessions. This is a fundamental tenet of Judaism? If a person covets someone else's donkey, he can't be a good Jew? If a person covets someone else's car, he can't be a good Jew? Why did Hashem include jealousy in the Ten Commandments along with faith and idolatry and Shabbos observance? Is it really so fundamental to Judaism?

That's right! The answer is a resounding yes. Jealousy is the exact opposite of faith. "Don't be jealous" tells us that Hashem controls the world. "Don't be jealous" tells us that Hashem cares. "Don't be jealous" tells us that Hashem is interested in each of us. "Don't be jealous" tells us that Hashem sits down every Rosh Hashanah and decides how much money each of us should make this year. "Don't be jealous" tells us that Hashem decides what kind of year each of us will have. This is fundamental to Judaism. This is vital to Judaism.

The *Aseres Hadibros* begin with *emunah* in theory, but they end with *emunah* in practice. *Lo sachmod.* Don't be jealous. That's *emunah* in practice. Don't be jealous of your neighbor's wife, because the wife He gave you is one He wants *you* to have as a life partner. Don't be jealous of your neighbor's house, because the house He gave to you is the one in which He wants you to live. Don't be jealous of your neighbor's donkey, because that donkey is meant to be that person's donkey, not yours.

That's what *emunah* is all about. And if we put this into practice, our daily lives would be transformed.

All parents and teachers know that no one standard applies to all children. Teachers know that they can't demand the same type of performance from everyone in the classroom. They can't set up a contest and demand that everyone learn an entire *perek* by heart. We can't demand that from everyone. Children have to be taught to be satisfied with performing according to their own talents and abilities.

Some people have been known to disagree with this point of view, basing their opinion on the Gemara (*Bava Basra* 22a), which tells us, "*Kin'as sofrim tarbeh chachmah.* Envy among students proliferates wisdom." They infer from this that competition is to be desired because it brings about an increase in the overall volume of learning.

But this is an incorrect interpretation of the Gemara. Competition does not mean that what one person does everyone else must also do. That is not a Jewish concept. Rather, the Gemara is telling us that if one child in the classroom exerts himself to memorize an entire chapter, the rest of the class will be inspired to exert themselves to the limits of their own particular abilities and accomplish the most they possibly can.

Rav Aharon Feldman once related that when he first came to Yeshivas Rabbeinu Chaim Berlin, Rav Yitzchak Hutner, the famous *Rosh Yeshivah,* asked him, "So what do you think of the *yeshivah*?"

"This *yeshivah* is unlike any I've ever seen before," he replied with not inconsiderable temerity. "It seems that in this *yeshivah* a person can get recognition even if he isn't the best learner. I've never seen such a *yeshivah.* In other *yeshivos,* excellence is measured by outstanding learning. But what kind of *yeshivah* gives recognition to someone who does not excel in learning?"

"You know what kind of *yeshivah* it is?" Rav Hutner told him. "It's the kind of *yeshivah* I want to have. It's the kind of a *yeshivah* in which a person can know that if he has certain talents and uses them he will get recognition. It's the kind of *yeshivah* where everyone can reach a level of excellence. It's the kind of *yeshivah* I want to have." In Chaim Berlin, if there was a boy with musical talent, he would sit next to Rav Hutner at his Purim table and play the violin. And he would feel like a million dollars.

We have to deal with our children as individuals. As one psychologist put it, if the only tool that we have is a hammer, then every problem in the world becomes a nail. But not every problem in the world is a nail. Parents and educators must have toolboxes that contain many tools. We must teach the children that they are infinitely worthy for themselves, no matter what their abilities are. The people with lesser talents and abilities are not Hashem's mistakes, Heaven forbid. Hashem created each person exactly as he is and gave him a mission in life according to those abilities. Our educational system would be vastly improved if we understood this.

The business world would also be vastly improved if we understood that competition is really futile; that Hashem decides on Rosh Hashanah how much we're each going to make, that what we do will not affect what we or others will make during the year. If we understood this, our attitudes towards business would be much more positive.

A man once wanted to get into a certain line of business. He went to his friends and relatives who were in the same line and said, "Listen, I'd like to get into your line of business. Can you give me some customers and leads?"

At every turn, the man was rebuffed. "What, I should give you my customers?" was the typical reply. "And what's going to be with my business?"

Finally, he approached Rav Moshe Mordechai Heschel, who was later to become the Kopichenitzer Rebbe. "No problem," said Rav Moshe Mordechai. "Here, take my customer list."

The man was stunned. "You're giving me the whole list? What's going to be with your business?"

"Don't worry about it," Rav Moshe Mordechai replied. "Do you think Hashem doesn't have enough *parnassah* for the both of us?"

I once told this story to someone, and he advised me not to repeat it when I speak in public. Only a future *rebbe* could do something like that, but ordinary people would never relate to it. But I didn't take this advice, and I did repeat this story in public.

One day, a simple Jew in Baltimore came over to me and told me that a similar thing had happened to him. He had an established electronics business, and someone had asked him for help in starting a similar business.

"So I gave him my Rolodex," said the man. "It helped him get started and he's quite successful now. By the way, my own business didn't suffer one iota."

How's that for ordinary Jewish people? Never underestimate what a Jew can do if he is properly educated.

A business man once came running to Rav Meir Premishlaner. "Rebbe, help me. Someone is opening a business like mine right down down the street from me. What's gonna be? *Oy gevald!* I'm going to lose all my business."

"Calm down, my friend," said Rav Meir Premishlaner. "Tell me, have you ever noticed that before a horse drinks from a pond or a river he always stamps on the ground first? Do you know why? Because when the horse sees his reflection in the pond, he thinks there's another horse there. So he tries to chase him away. Don't worry about this other business. The threat to you is just a figment of your imagination."

A Jewish jeweler in Antwerp, Belgium, once came to Rav Chaim Kreiswirth, the *rav* of the city. "I don't understand it," he told Rav Kreiswirth. "The man across the street is doing twice the business I am. What am I doing wrong?"

"How much square footage do you have?" asked Rav Kreiswirth, thinking the other man might have a bigger store.

The man shook his head. "No, that's not it. I checked it out, and we both have the same square footage."

"How about the lighting?" asked Rav Kreiswirth. "Maybe he has better lighting. Lighting is very important in the jewelry business, you know."

The man shook his head again. "No, we have the same type of lighting."

"Well, maybe he just has better goods than you do," suggested Rav Kreiswirth.

"No," said the man. "We both have the same supplier."

"How many customers come to his store each day?" asked Rav Kreiswirth.

"Well, I know that he has twice the number of customers I do."

"Aha!" said Rav Kreiswirth. "Now I know what you're doing wrong. Every day your friend across the street comes into his store and minds his business. But every day you come into your store, you're looking across the street. You, my friend, are minding two stores at the same time. It's no wonder that you're not doing as well."

Ours would be a different world if people really believed in Hashem, if they realized that *everything* is in Hashem's hands. It's a matter of faith. It's a matter of *emunah*.

Let us return now to the problem of what to tell your children when they tell you that all the other kids are going to Florida for midwinter break. So what can you tell them? Are you going to tell them, "No, you can't go because it's a matter of faith"? Are you going to say, "Believe and you won't be jealous"?

I hate to disappoint you, but that's not going to work.

If you start talking about faith when they come for the Florida trip or the new car or whatever it is that they come for, it's just not going to work. If you first start talking about faith at crunch time, don't expect to be successful.

Faith in Hashem has to be one of the constant themes of our homes. It has to be discussed often at our kitchen tables and our dining room tables. Our children have to hear from us constantly that there's a Father in Heaven Who takes care of us. When we suffer setbacks, be they personal, financial, medical or any of the other trials and tribulations that make up the fabric of life, our children should constantly hear from us, "Listen, Hashem has helped us until now, and He will continue to help us in the future." Hashem has to be a reality in our lives. Our children must hear from us that Hashem has a role for us and a place for each and every one of us.

Then when they hear they cannot go to Florida, it may be a little tough for them to swallow, but they will be able to deal with it. "No, you can't go to Florida," you have to tell them, "because we can't afford it. We don't always look at what other people have and do. That's not the way we do things in this home." They'll know where you're coming from and they'll respect you for it. But only if that is really the way you live.

When you want to buy a car, do you look out the window to see what kind of car your neighbor is driving? When you want to go on vacation, do you want to know where your neighbor went on vacation? Do you try to keep up with the Joneses or the Cohenses? If the answer to all these questions is no, then you have a very good chance with your children.

Let us take one more look at the last of the *Aseres Hadibros*, the prohibition of *lo sachmod*. The Torah lists all that we should not covet, our friend's wife, his house, his donkey and so on, and the Torah concludes, "*Vechal asher lerei'echa*, nor anything that your friend may possess." What does the Torah mean by this? asked the Satmar Rav.

Every person, explains the Satmar Rav, has his own *peckel*, his own little bundle of grief. No matter how fortunate he may appear to the world, you can rest assured that his life is far from a bed of roses. So why should you covet the things your friend has? If you want to take what your friend has, you would have to take "all that your friend possesses," the whole package, all the pain and sorrow as well.

There is an old saying that if every person put his or her *peckel* out on a table, and had the choice of taking back any *peckel* they want, each person would take back his own *peckel*. Life is a package deal, good and bad, and in the final analysis, everyone is most comfortable with his own package.

The first time I heard that saying was at a concert to benefit HASC, the Hebrew Academy for Special Children. A 14-year-old boy got up in front of 3,000 people and spoke about what it was like to have an emotionally disturbed brother. He described the terrible strain on the family, the difficulties, the disruption of the household. And he spoke of how HASC had helped this child immeasurably.

As the boy was delivering this most moving speech, he coughed and coughed constantly. "You'll have to excuse my cough," the boy said. "You see, I have cystic fibrosis. But it's all right. When everyone puts everything on the table, you usually take back your own *peckel*. This is mine."

This is the bottom line. Hashem put us here, and He gave each and every one of us a *peckel* to get us through life, to find the fulfillment for which we are destined. It's a matter of faith.

We say every morning, "*Baruch Atah Hashem Elokeinu Melech Haolam she'asah li kol tzorki*. Blessed are You, Hashem our Lord, King of the Universe, Who has prepared for me all my needs." Let us think deeply about these words. Let us realize that if Hashem has indeed given us everything we need there is no reason to be jealous of anything or anyone else.

The Tip of the Iceberg

I F YOU HAVE EVER BEEN ON A DIET, YOU WILL UNDERSTAND exactly what I mean. You can try this kind of diet or that one. You can spend three months eating only grapefruit and another three months eating only chicken and eggs. You may even lose weight in the process. But in the long run, it's not going to work. As soon as you go off the diet, you gain back the weight you lost and then some.

Dieting alone is not the answer. You also need behavior modification. You have to change your whole outlook on food. It's simply not enough to stop eating for a while. You also have to change the eating habits that got you into trouble in the first place.

The same applies in even greater measure to improving our *bein adam lachaveiro*, our relationships with other people. Over the last few years, we have seen a sea change in the Jewish community worldwide. Jewish people every-where have been making a tremendous effort to improve their *bein adam lachaveiro*. People are devoting more time and energy to *chessed* projects and working hard to combat *lashon hara*.

There are many aspects to *bein adam lachaveiro*, but I believe that there is one *mitzvah* which is fundamental to them all. If we concentrate on this one *mitzvah*, we will become better people, better friends, better spouses. We will become better Jews. What is this potent *mitzvah*? It is the *mitzvas asei de'oraisa* of *betzedek tishpot amisecha*. The Torah demands that we judge every person generously, fair-ly and kindly. We have to be *dan lekaf zchus*, to give the ben-efit of the doubt. If we master this one *mitzvah*, everything else falls into place.

How do we know that this *mitzvah* is so fundamental? All you have to do is open a *Chumash* and it jumps out at you.

Listen to these four consecutive *pessukim*. Judge others fairly (*Vayikra* 19:15). Don't speak *lashon hara* (*Vayikra* 19:16). Don't stand by idly when your friend is in danger (*Vayikra* 19:17). Do not hate your friend; do not embarrass or humiliate somebody publicly; do not take revenge; love others as you love yourself (*Vayikra* 19:18). That is it. These four *pessukim* encompass virtually the entire galaxy of *bein adam lachaveiro*. Don't hate people. Don't take revenge. Don't humiliate people. Don't embarrass people. Don't speak *lashon hara*. Care about other people, and eventually you will come to love them.

But how does it all begin? It begins with three words. *Betzedek tishpot amisecha*. Give people the benefit of the doubt. The Torah is telling us that if we give them the bene-fit of the doubt we won't speak *lashon hara*. We won't hate them. We won't want revenge. We'll have no need to embar-rass them publicly. Give them the benefit of the doubt, and everything else will fall by the wayside.

"The more you give the benefit of the doubt," writes the

Chafetz Chaim, "the less *lashon hara* you'll speak." It's an equation. And they are inversely proportional. The more you give the benefit of the doubt, the less *lashon hara* you will speak. The less you give the benefit of the doubt, the more *lashon hara* you will speak. Think about it. That's how it all starts.

Some time ago, we had the good fortune to marry off a son. My wife and I made up the guest list and sent out invitations. A few nights before the *chasunah*, we sat down to make a seating plan. As we were going over the list I noticed that a certain friend of ours who lives in Brooklyn had never responded.

"I don't understand why he never sent back his reply card," I said to my wife. "You know, he claims to be a good friend. He tells me all the time that he feels very close to me. Why didn't he send back his reply card?"

That was the extent of the conversation. I stopped just short of falling into the trap of *lashon hara*.

At the *chasunah*, I mentioned to the man's son, who lives in Baltimore, that his father had never responded to the invitation. He seemed surprised.

The next day, I get a call from this man. "You know," he said, "I never got an invitation to the *chasunah*."

"It's okay," I said. "It would have been nice to have you."

And that was how we left it — no acrimony, no recriminations.

A week later, the man called back. "I just got the invitation," he said. "It's postmarked Baltimore, Maryland, February 10." He received it on March 23. It took six weeks for it to travel from Baltimore to Brooklyn.

Baruch Hashem, we did not speak *lashon hara* about him, but we easily could have questioned his friendship and his gratitude for everything we had done for him, which was considerable. We could easily have raked him over the coals. And why? Because we didn't give him the benefit of the doubt. We didn't say to each other that the invitation probably got lost in the mail. There's no *mitzvah* to give the United States Postal Service the benefit of the doubt, but there certainly is a *mitzvah* to give another Jew the benefit of the doubt.

This was exactly what the Chafetz Chaim meant. Most *lashon hara* starts with a judgment, a character assessment. Why? Why did he do this? Why did he do that? And that leads to *lashon hara*. It is just one short step from character assessment to character assassination.

The Torah tells us that the Jewish people had to remain in the Wilderness for 40 years because of the 40 days the *meraglim* spent scouting *Eretz Yisrael* — one year for each day.

Rav Chaim Shmulevitz is puzzled by this. Did the *meraglim* speak *lashon hara* about *Eretz Yisrael* for 40 days? They probably didn't even speak *lashon hara* for 40 minutes. Why then were the Jewish people punished for the entire 40 days the *meraglim* were away?

True, says Rav Chaim Shmulevitz, there were no 40 days of *lashon hara*. But there was 40 days of judgments; 40 days of assessments; 40 days of jumping to conclusions. And that is where *lashon hara* begins. Making judgments leads to *lashon hara*. Giving the benefit of the doubt leads away from *lashon hara*.

The Mishnah in *Avos* tells us, "*Hevei dan es kol ha'adam lekaf zchus.*" What exactly do these words mean? The popular translation is "give all people the benefit of the doubt." But that is not completely accurate. The phrase for "all people" is *kol adam*. The phrase *kol ha'adam*, with the definite article, has a different connotation. It means "the entire person." Give the entire person the benefit of the doubt.

A very subtle and important message is implicit in these words. You cannot judge a person fairly and accurately until you know the entire person. And that is practically impossible. Every person is an entire universe unto himself, with a singular past, present and future, with undisclosed memories, thoughts and dreams, with complex histories and historic complexes. What do we really know about other people? What do we know about their familial relationships, their childhoods, their aspirations? The truth is that we know next to nothing, just the tiny tip of the iceberg that shows above the surface.

Trying to read a person is like opening a 400-page book to page 253 and starting to read. Go figure out who the characters are, what motivates them, what led up to the current state of affairs. It is useless.

It is just as useless to try to figure out what another person is really all about. Therefore, since you cannot judge the "entire person," you cannot judge at all.

Several years ago my wife, my daughter and I went on a three-day vacation to the White Mountains in New Hampshire. High up in the mountains, in a Chassidic summer colony situated in a hamlet with the incongruous name of Bethlehem, there is an old hotel which houses a restaurant. Believe me, it is a real pleasure to be able to come to New Hampshire and enjoy a delicious *heimishe* meal. I called up and made reservations for the three of us for all three days.

Our first evening in New Hampshire, we check into our rooms and go straight to the restaurant. The waiter, who apparently speaks only Yiddish, asks us our names. Then he pulls a scrap of paper from his pocket and squints at it. Can't find the name Frand. But there's something else there with an F. He shrugs. Good enough. He seats us at this reserved table and takes our orders.

Ten minutes into our meal, another group of three comes in — husband, wife and teenaged son, Chassidic people in full regalia. They also have reservations for three, and their name also begins with an F.

The waiter is not fazed. "We have room," he says. "You sit right over there."

"I'm sorry," the woman says to the waiter in a low but very firm voice. "I would like that table over there." She was referring, of course, to our table. "I reserved that table specifically.

You promised me that table, and that is the table I want."

This is a little beyond the training of the waiter, and he gets flustered. Who can blame him? He goes into the kitchen and returns with the proprietress.

The woman repeats her demand to the proprietress, speaking in hushed tones to save us the embarrassment, but nonetheless, I hear what's going on.

I see this woman is really taking it to heart, so why not be magnanimous? "We don't mind moving to a different table," I said. "It's no problem."

"Ach!" she says. "Heaven forbid. I won't let you move after you've begun your meal. You're staying right there."

That puts a quick and effective end to my involvement in the negotiations. I go back to minding my own business. But inside, I can't help wondering about this fussy woman. "Why doesn't this lady get a life?" I think to myself. "It's only a table."

Finally, the proprietress seats them at another table. We finish our meal. They finish theirs. The men go to the back room for Minchah, which is just about to start. The women retire to the porch, where this interesting woman strikes up a conversation with my wife.

"So what's your name?" she asks.

"Frand," my wife replies.

"Really? Are you related to Rabbi Frand from Baltimore?"

"My husband."

"Really?"

A month or two later, I get a call from this woman. She is involved with a *tzedakah* and wants me to come speak. After speaking with her for a few minutes about her project, I am thoroughly mystified. She seems quite intelligent and normal. Why would she make a grand fuss about a table in a restaurant?

I can't help myself. "I'd like to ask you a question."

"Sure, why not?"

"Do you remember that evening in New Hampshire?"

"How could I forget?"

"You know, I couldn't help overhearing your conversation with the waiter and the owner about that table you reserved."

"Really? I feel so bad. I didn't want you to hear. It was so embarrassing, wasn't it?"

"A little," I say. "What was it about that table? Why was it so important?"

"Really? You want to know? I'll tell you. You know we're *Chassidishe* people, don't you? My husband and my son are uncomfortable with the way some women dress in the summer. It makes it very hard for us to go anywhere. We came to New Hampshire because it's not as crowded as the Catskills. We always choose that table, because two of the seats face the wall. My husband and son don't have to worry about who is going to walk into the restaurant while they're eating. You never can tell what kind of people are going to come in, can you?"

Now, who would have thought of that? Here I thought she was a little deranged, and she was really a scrupulous Jewish woman trying to protect the sanctity of her family. How was I supposed to know that? I apologized to her for not giving her the benefit of the doubt. I should have. I didn't know the entire story or the entire person. What right did I have to judge?

Fine, so I had my brush with not giving the benefit of the doubt. I learned my lesson, and I'm cured. Right? Wrong. Somehow, it doesn't quite work out that way. We've all been told from early childhood to give everyone the benefit of the doubt. It's been drilled into us by our kindergarten teachers, by our *rabbeim*, by our *roshei yeshivah* and *rebbetzins*. And still, we never learn. We keep on making the same mistakes over and over and over again.

Let me tell you a parable.

A young fellow is given a small part in a play — a very small part. A tiny part. All he has to do is say these six words when he hears the cannon go off: "Hark, I hear the cannon roar." That is his entire part. The cannon booms, and he's supposed to say, "Hark, I hear the cannon roar."

For two weeks, this young fellow practices his part over and over again. "Hark, I hear the cannon roar. Hark, I hear the cannon roar. Hark, I hear the cannon roar." He has it down cold.

At long last, the great day arrives. The curtain rises, and the fellow is onstage. The cannon booms, and he cries out, "Hey, what in the world was that?"

Cute story — and a very important message. No matter how much we practice our part, when the reality pops up on us, we are likely to flub our lines. And that is exactly what happened to me.

I had my comeuppance with the table in New Hampshire, and afterwards, I spoke about giving the benefit of the doubt in different communities all over the country. I was really sensitized to the subject.

One day, I walked into the bank to get some important papers from my safe-deposit box. As in most banks, the boxes are kept in a vault with a bank employee in attendance to sign you in and out.

When I arrived, the bank clerk was on the telephone speaking Russian. I waited for her to get off, but she just kept on talking. I cleared my throat loudly. She gave me a brief glance, raised one finger and kept right on talking.

I was losing my patience. Was this a way to treat a customer? What right did she have to make me wait while she spoke to her family or friends on the telephone? She certainly wouldn't be doing this if she were sitting in the main lobby in full earshot of everyone else. But here, in the privacy of the vault, she was not accountable. Maybe that's the way they treat people back in Russia, but this was the good old USA. Customers are supposed to be treated with courtesy and respect. These and other thoughts of this ilk passed through my mind as I waited for the Russian chitchat to come to an end.

Finally, she hung up the telephone, apologized and gave me my box. I went into one of the private little cubicles and retrieved the papers I needed. To my dismay, when I came out to return the box, she was back on the telephone, speaking in Russian once again. Once again, I had to cool my heels while she conversed with her people. I was very upset. How unprofessional! But what was I supposed to do? Complain to the management?

Just then, who should appear but the manager of the bank herself. She listened for a minute or two to the woman speaking in Russian, then she started to question her. It suddenly became very clear that she had not been talking to friends and family at all. A customer in another branch of the bank, an elderly lady who spoke only Russian, was having a serious problem with an account. No one else could communicate with this distraught, culture-shocked old lady from Russia except for the vault attendant in my branch, and she was doing her best to be helpful. I had certainly misjudged this fine lady.

So there it is. After all this practice and awareness, I should have been able to say, "Hark, I hear the cannon roar," but I flubbed the lines. I did not give her the benefit of the doubt.

Another insight into the particular language of that *mishnah*: There are situations, of course, in which you really do not have to give the benefit of the doubt — because there is no doubt. Rabbeinu Yonah and the Chafetz Chaim say that when we are dealing with repeat offenders, with people that have a record of doing a particular misdeed repeatedly, we can suspect the worst. If the checks a certain person gives you always bounce, you do not have to give him the benefit of the doubt. In fact, you would be wise not to trust him any longer.

Unfortunately, there are abusive people in the world — abusive parents, abusive spouses, abusive children, abusive friends. If anyone has an established track record for being abusive, you do not have to give him the benefit of the doubt. Then there is no doubt. You know what he is going to do.

Nonetheless, that does not give you the right to write off the entire person. Just because a person may have one or two faults, you can't suspect and accuse him of anything and everything. You have to judge the "entire person." You have to see him as a many-sided person, which he is. And you have to judge him fairly and give him the benefit of the doubt in every single area where he has not proven himself flawed.

We all know such people: wonderful people in every way, except that they are always late, or always untidy, or always grumpy in the morning. People can have one flaw yet be wonderful in every other way. Therefore, when you find a flaw in a person, you must still give him the benefit of the doubt and assume he is wonderful in every other way.

If we do this, if we give everyone the benefit of the doubt, if we recognize that we cannot begin to fathom the entire person, then we will not speak *lashon hara*. We will not hate or humiliate or take vengeance on another person. As the Chafetz Chaim says, if we give everyone the benefit of the doubt we would radically improve our *bein adam lachaveiro*. We would have superb relationships with other people.

Furthermore, we would also vastly improve our *bein adam laMakom*, our relationship with Hashem. The Gemara tells us (*Shabbos* 127b) that if we give others the benefit of the doubt we will be given the benefit of the doubt when we are judged in Heaven. What can this possibly mean? asks the Sfas Emes. Hashem will give us the benefit of the doubt? Hashem has doubts? Hashem has doubts about the details of the story? Hashem has doubts about our inner thoughts and motivations? Ridiculous. What then does this Gemara mean?

The Gemara is saying something else altogether, says the Chafetz Chaim. If we judge others favorably, generously and kindly, Hashem will also judge favorably, generously and kindly after our lives are over and we come before the Heavenly Court.

What exactly does this mean? Let me explain.

I'm a *rebbi* by profession. From time to time, I give tests, and then I have to grade them. I am what's called an easy grader. If the answer is basically correct, even if it is slightly off in some of the details, I will give at least partial credit. Some *rabbeim* and teachers, however, are strict graders, very strict graders. If an answer is not perfect, they give no credit for it whatsoever.

What kind of grader is Hashem? When He marks the final examinations called our lives, is He an easy grader or a strict grader? The answer to this question is that it depends. It depends on us. If we ourselves were easy graders, if we judged people generously, fairly and kindly, He will be an easy grader with us as well. But if we were strict graders, if we were relentless and merciless with other people, never giving them the benefit of the doubt, He will do the same with us, Heaven forbid.

And let me tell you, if Hashem judges people strictly, they don't stand a chance. Let's take *tefillah*. We go to *shul* three times a day. We say all our *tefillos*. And we think we're doing fine. But Hashem takes one look at it and says, "That's called prayer? During Shacharis, you think about what you are going to do in business that day. During Minchah, you think about what you did in business that day. And during Maariv, you think about what you are going to do in business tomorrow. This you call *tefillah*?"

No credit.

It's the same with all other *mitzvos*. If we start taking them apart and scrutinizing them closely, they all turn up flawed.

So what can we do? There is only one choice. Be kind and compassionate, generous and forgiving when you judge people. Then Hashem will do the same for us. The way we judge others determines the way we ourselves are judged.

The Baal Shem Tov takes this concept one step further. The Mishnah in *Avos* tells us, "*Al tadin es chavercha ad shetagia limkomo.*" What does this mean? The conventional translation is "do not judge your friend until you stand in his place." But the Baal Shem Tov offers an alternative interpretation. "You will become your own judge when you encounter your friend's situation."

Hashem will sometimes let a person be his own judge, he explains, and that is a very frightening thing. Hashem decides not to pass on him. Instead, he allows him to see another person doing something similar to what he did. Then Hashem waits to see how he handles it. If he judges harshly, Hashem turns his own judgment back on him, and he stands accused and condemned by his own words. But if he judges kindly, then he too benefits from the leniency of his own judgment.

We find exactly such a story in *Tanach*. David Hamelech sent Uriah to the battlefront, where he is killed, and David subsequently married his widow Batsheva. Although David did not violate any laws of the Torah, Hashem disapproved of his action. It was beneath the dignity of a king to do such a thing.

So Hashem sent Nassan Hanavi to put David to the test. "What would you say about the following situation?" Nassan asked David. "There was a poor man who had only one little lamb. And there was a very wealthy man who many lambs. Then the wealthy man decided he wanted the poor man's lamb as well, and he took it. What would you say about such a person?"

"He deserves to die," David replied.

"*Atah ha'ish!*" You are that man!" declared Nassan. "You had so many lambs. Why did you take Uriah's lamb as well?"

What utterly dreadful, terrible words! How devastating to be condemned by one's own words. *Atah ha'ish!* You are the one!

Sometimes, you will be the judge. Sometimes, you will judge your entire lifetime. You certainly don't want your own words coming back to haunt you. After all, how can you defend yourself against your own accusation?

So we have our work cut out for us. We know that we hold our own fate in our hands, that by giving other people the benefit of the doubt, by judging them kindly and fairly, we stand to gain everything both in *bein adam lachaveiro* and *bein adam laMakom*. But still, what do you do when someone says something really nasty to you for no reason whatsoever? How do you give a person the benefit of the doubt when he does something vile, vicious and hurtful? How do you excuse the inexcusable?

The answer is pain. When people are in pain, when they are in distress, when they are under pressure, they are not responsible for what they say or do. Even if what they said was undeniably nasty, even if what they did was undeniably vile, they are not accountable if they are suffering.

The Gemara (*Bava Basra* 16b) tells us that "a person is not responsible for what he does in times of suffering." Even when Iyov said inappropriate things, Hashem did not hold it against him. A person in pain is not accountable.

Unfortunately, there is a lot of suffering out there in the world. There is pain. There is worry. There is frustration. People have health problems. They have problems with their children. They have *shidduchim* worries. They have problems earning a living. People are under a lot of pressure, and when people are under pressure, they sometimes say or do terrible things.

Let me tell you a story about a man whose funeral I attended some time ago. One of the relatives told this story in his eulogy.

The man was an *ehrlicher Yid*, an honest Jew. He grew up in Pittsburgh during the Depression and was drafted in the Second World War. At the tender age of 20, he was the only Jewish boy on an army base in the Philippines. To his eternal credit, he remained strong in his *Yiddishkeit*, a really fine Jewish boy.

One day, a Jewish pilot was shot down. His body was brought to the army base for burial, but there was no Jewish chaplain. In fact, there was no one Jewish at all, except for this young boy from Pittsburgh.

They asked him to say some prayers for the dead pilot, and he did. Then they asked him to give the pilot a Jewish burial.

Imagine the situation. A boy barely out of his teen years, 10,000 miles away from home, was asked to do a *taharah* and a *kevurah*. Somehow, he managed to give the pilot a proper Jewish burial.

After the war, he returned home and decided to look up the pilot's parents who lived in the Bronx. In 1945, this was no easy matter. He took a bus from Pittsburgh to New York, then a subway up to the Bronx. He found their apartment and knocked on the door. The pilot's father opened it.

"Can I come in?" he said.

"Who are you?" asked the pilot's father.

"I was in the Philippines," he replied, "when your son's body was brought to the base. I was the only Jew there and they asked me to take care of the burial. I wanted to tell you about it. I thought you would ... "

The door slammed in his face in midsentence, and he was left standing in the hallway all by himself.

What did he say when he returned to Pittsburgh and his family asked him what had happened? Did he consider the pilot's father rude? Ungrateful for everything he had done? Not at all. "It must be too painful," he told his family. "It must be too painful for them to hear about the precious son they lost."

A young man once asked Rav Chaim Ozer Grodzinski, the *gadol hador* in Europe before the war, to help his father secure a rabbinical position in a small community. His father was in a difficult financial situation, and the position was very important to him. He wanted Rav Chaim Ozer to write a letter to the community on behalf of his father. Rav Chaim Ozer, for whatever reason, did not feel that the young man's father was a suitable candidate, and he declined to get involved.

The young man flew into a rage. He started yelling at Rav Chaim Ozer, the *gadol hador*, but Rav Chaim Ozer sat there silently. He did not respond to the outrageous outburst. Afterwards, he was asked why he accepted abuse from the young man without even the slightest reprimand. "He's worried about his father," said Rav Chaim Ozer said. "His father needs a position. He needs to make a living. The young man was not responsible."

That's what we have to say, and that's what we have to think. If we can't tell ourselves that we don't know the whole story, we have to tell ourselves that the person must have been in pain or worried or frustrated.

But what if that also doesn't work? What if the person doesn't seem to be suffering in any way?

Even so, we must give him the benefit of the doubt without any rationalization whatsoever. We must bow to the wisdom of the Torah that commands us to give the benefit of the doubt always, even if we cannot find any excuses at all with our limited intelligence. Just because we cannot find it doesn't mean that a reason does not exist. Maybe we're just not smart enough.

There's a terrific book on the subject called *The Other Side of the Story*. I recommend it highly. At the end of the book, there's a beautiful *tefillah*, copied from the wall of *Kever Rachel,* imploring Hashem to help us see the good in everyone.

It set me to wondering, however. Why out of all possible *tefillos* is this particular *tefillah* etched onto the wall of *Kever Rachel?*

Rabbi Yakov Luban offered the following insight. *Kever Rachel* actually does represent the concept of giving the benefit of the doubt. Rashi writes that when Yaakov Avinu asked Yosef to bring him to burial in *Eretz Yisrael*, he addressed an old sore point. Yosef had always harbored some resentment against his father for burying his mother Rachel by the roadside. All these years, Yaakov had not found it necessary to justify his actions to his young son, but now that he wanted a favor, he felt he owed him an explanation.

Hashem had him bury her there because a thousand years later, when the Jewish people would be led into Babylonian exile, they would pass her gravesite, and she would pray for them. "Rachel will cry for her children." Yosef could not have known this reason unless it was revealed to him through *ruach hakodesh*. But there was a reason nonetheless. He should have given his father the benefit of the doubt.

It all comes down to one thing. No matter what we see, no matter what we perceive, no matter what we think, we are only aware of the tip of the iceberg, that small peak that breaks through the surface.

But what about the bulk of the iceberg under the surface? Are there additional details to the story? Are there additional facets to the person we are judging? Are there mitigating circumstances? Are there unfathomable explanations?

We cannot possibly know.

One thing is certain. We cannot pass judgment on an iceberg if we've only seen its tip.

And Nothing
But The Truth

FOR SHEER DRAMA, THE REUNION OF YOSEF AND HIS brothers probably has no equal in the Torah. One moment, they are arguing with the fearsome Egyptian viceroy, fighting for their freedom and their lives. The next moment, he reveals himself as their long-lost brother Yosef, whom they had sold into captivity 22 years earlier.

"I am Yosef!" he exclaims. "Is my father still alive?"

The brothers recoil in shock and speechless dismay.

The Midrash offers a very famous comment on Yosef's declaration. "*Oy lanu miyom hadin, oy lanu miyom hatochachah.* Woe to us on the day of judgment, woe to us on the day of rebuke."

The commentators are puzzled. Where is the judgment? Where is the rebuke? All Yosef did was reveal his identity and ask about his father.

The answer, some commentators suggest, is that being forced to face the truth is the most powerful form of rebuke. Sometimes the truth is crushing.

Yosef's brothers had considered him a *rodef*, a predator seeking to destroy them. They sat in judgment on him and concluded that he deserved to die. As an act of last-minute leniency, they sold him into slavery, and they walked away, secure in the justice of what they had done. For 22 years, whenever they thought about their missing brother, they reassured themselves that he was to blame for his own fate. He was evil, and they were just. They had done the right thing.

All of a sudden, they were faced with the horrifying but undeniable truth. "I am Yosef!" This dreaded viceroy, who held their lives in his hands, who could have snuffed out their lives at his slightest whim without anyone voicing a word of protest, this dreaded viceroy was actually Yosef. If he was really intent on killing them, why hadn't he done so? Then the awful truth dawned on them. They had been wrong; horribly, unforgivably wrong. Yosef had never meant them harm. They were wrong, and he was right. That was the sharpest rebuke of all. The realization that they had lived a lie for 22 years was crushing. Woe to us on the day of judgment, comments the Midrash, woe to us on the day of rebuke.

If we look closely, this thought is explicit in the *passuk*. "*Aval asheimim anachnu*," the brothers said. "We are indeed guilty." The word *aval* ordinarily translates as "but" or "nonetheless," but in this instance, it means "indeed" or "it is true." They faced the awful truth, and acknowledged their guilt.

The Rambam writes that the essence of the *Viduy* we say on Yom Kippur is the three-word phrase *aval anachnu chatanu*. Traditionally, these words mean "but we have sinned." But we can also see here a reference to Yosef's brothers. *Aval anachnu chatanu*. Indeed, we have sinned. When we take stock of our lives on Yom Kippur and face the truth, we cannot help but say, "Indeed, we have sinned. It is true! We have allowed ourselves to be distracted by foolish-ness and temptation. It is true. We have sinned." The truth is our greatest rebuke, just as it was the crushing rebuke to Yosef's brothers.

The Gemara tells us (*Nedarim* 8b), "There will be no *Gehinnom* in the next world. Rather, the Holy One, Blessed Is He, will unveil the sun. The righteous will be healed by it, and the sinful will be punished by it."

Rabbi Zev Leff of Yerushalayim explains that the sun in this allegory is a metaphor for the light of the truth. In the future, Hashem will shed the light of truth upon the world. There will be no more subterfuges, no more excuses, no more dissimulation, only the unadorned truth. There will be no place to hide, and we will have to face the truth. The righteous will be vindicated by the truth, but the sinful will be condemned by it.

At that time, we will all look back over the long span of our lifetimes, and we will understand what our lives really meant. And if we discover, Heaven forbid, that for all those years we were living a lie, it will be incredibly painful, more painful than any external rebuke could possibly be.

There was once an executive who worked in middle-level management for a small but prestigious company. He was very devoted to the company and did everything in his power to climb the corporate ladder.

One day, without any forewarning whatsoever, the com-pany went out of business. The decision to liquidate had been made behind closed doors in utmost secrecy and was immediately implemented. One day it was business as usual, and the next day all the employees were asked to clear out their desks and seek employment elsewhere.

A security guard was posted at the door to make sure the employees took nothing belonging to the company — no calculators, no equipment, no supplies, no files, no records. Nothing but personal belongings.

When it was the executive's turn to pass through security,

he walked right past the guard and headed for the door.

"Excuse me, sir," the security guard called to him. "I have to inspect your box. I have to make sure it contains nothing belonging to the company."

The executive spun around in a rage. He put down his box, ripped open his shirt and bared his chest.

"You want to see what belongs to the company?" he cried out, pounding his chest. "This belongs to the company. My heart! I gave 30 years of my life to the company. I was here day and night, and holidays, too. I gave the company every-thing. And suddenly you just go out of business? For this I gave my life? For this I have to suffer the indignity of being treated like a thief? You're worried that I might take some pencils, but what about my heart? What about the best years of my life?"

What had pierced this man so deeply? Was it the loss of his job, his prestigious position, his retirement benefits? No. It was much more than that.

All of a sudden, this poor man had been hit with the awful truth. All of a sudden, he realized that all the time he had stolen from his family — all the weekends he had spent in the office, all the nights he had spent with clients — were all for nothing. How could he have done this to himself and his family? How could he have frittered away the best years of his life for a mirage? How could he have allowed himself to live a lie? The awful truth stared him in the face, and it was more painful than he could bear.

How do we become conditioned to facing the truth? How do we avoid the nasty surprise of discovering we have been living a lie? Of discovering that we have wasted our lives away by deluding ourselves?

It all begins with our attitude to speaking truth. If we are scrupulous in the words we speak, making sure that we speak only the truth, then we are better able to recognize truth when it stares us in the face. But if we rationalize about the little falsehoods, the line between truth and falsehood becomes blurred in our minds. Then we can no longer differentiate truth from falsehood very easily, and we are missing the truth that stares us in the face.

In times gone by, there were people who knew the meaning of honesty, of truthfulness. There were people who cared about integrity of every word they uttered. There were people who were so superbly sensitized to the truth that they could not tolerate anything that smacked of falsehood.

Do you know when the Chafetz Chaim got *semichah*? Late in life, he applied for a passport to travel from Poland to *Eretz Yisrael*. The passport application asked for the applicant's profession, and the natural answer for the Chafetz Chaim was rabbi. There was only one problem. Although he had already written *Mishnah Berurah* and was acknowledged as the leading Halachic authority for all of *Klal Yisrael*, he had never received *semichah*.

If there was any person in the world who was entitled to call himself rabbi, it was the Chafetz Chaim. Yet he refused to do so, since it was not true. Officially, he was not a rabbi. So he sent a telegram to Rav Chaim Ozer Grodzinski in Vilna asking him for a *semichah* based on his works. Rav Chaim Ozer immediately telegraphed him a *semichah*, and the Chafetz Chaim was able to apply for a passport.

Amazing! Until the Chafetz Chaim had that telegram in his hands, he absolutely refused to represent himself as a rabbi, because technically, it was not true. Yet if you look in the telephone directories of some cities, you will find many hundreds upon hundreds of rabbis. Rav Eliahu Lopian, one of the most illustrious *tzaddikim* of the previous generation, used to be the *baal tefillah* for Mussaf on Rosh Hashanah and Yom Kippur every year until advanced old age. Traditionally, the *baal tefillah* first says a short paragraph of supplication, which begins with the following sentence, "*Hineni he'ani mimaas, nir'ash venifchad mipachad Yosheiv Tehilos Yisrael.* Here I am, the person of meager deeds, trembling and terrified by the terror of Hashem." Rav Eliahu

Lopian, however, would only say the first part of that sentence. He had no problem speaking of himself as a person of meager deeds. But trembling? Terrified? He couldn't bring himself to say those words about himself. For was he indeed atremble? Was he actually terrified? Not really, he believed. Then how could he utter an untruth? And so he omitted the second half of the sentence.

Let me tell you yet another story. The Chazon Ish and his brother-in-law Rav Shmuel Graineman once went to an early Minchah, which began 12:45. It turned out that there were exactly 10 people for the *minyan* with them included.

Just as they were about to start, Rav Shmuel turned to the Chazon Ish and said, "I just remembered that I made an appointment to meet someone at 1 o'clock. What should I do? If I want to make it in time for the appointment, I must leave now. But if I leave now, you won't have a *minyan* for Minchah."

"What's the question?" said the Chazon Ish. "Of course, you have to go right now. A word is a word. You told the man 1 o'clock, and you have to keep your word. Don't worry about the *minyan*."

These people understood the importance of truth. These people were incapable of letting a falsehood cross their lips.

The Gemara (*Bava Kama* 113b) implies that *geneivas daas*, deceitfulness, is worse than actual theft. Why is this so?

"Because speaking falsehood is an enormous transgression," Rabbeinu Yonah explains in *Shaarei Teshuvah*. "We are obligated to uphold the truth, because it is the one of the fundamental elements of the soul."

What are the building blocks of the soul? Of what material is the soul constructed? The Rabbeinu Yonah tells us the answer: Truth. The soul is made of truth. All souls are taken from beneath the *Kisei Hakavod*, the Divine Throne of Glory — from Hashem Himself, so to speak, and Hashem's seal is truth. Therefore, lying, cheating and deceiving are all antithetical to the soul. They are destructive.

In this light, we can understand Rabbeinu Yehudah Hachassid's advice in *Sefer Chassidim*. He writes that a person should do his best to avoid telling a lie even when the halachah permits doing so *mipnei hashalom*, for the sake of maintaining the peace. There may be no transgression in lying under such circumstances, but the lie is nevertheless destructive to the soul.

In our day and age, the standard of truthfulness has sunk to new lows. That is really not surprising. It is generally agreed that we live in the predawn of the Messianic age, and the Mishnah (*Sotah* 49b) tells us that one of the hallmarks of our age is the disappearance of truth. And indeed, if we look around contemporary society, we are struck by the total bankruptcy of truth.

Lying has become endemic to society. The public has become accustomed to having the government lie and then cover it up. According to the *Wall Street Journal*, 40 percent of all resumes are phony. A survey by the American Academy for the Advancement of Science has determined that 25 percent of scientists question the validity of data reported in scientific research papers. Lying is thoroughly pervasive in the business world, from the oft-repeated "the check is in the mail" to the guiding principle that determines policy by the likelihood of getting away with it.

Tragically, the disease of untruthfulness has infected the Jewish community as well. There was a time when the word of a Jewish person was sacrosanct. There was a time when people preferred to do business with observant Jews because they were assumed to be trustworthy. Is that still the case? Unfortunately, it is not.

Today, we hear Jews saying that they'd rather do business with gentiles than with other Jews. What a *chillul Hashem* this is!

The Sma writes that when Hashem finally brings the Jewish people back to *Eretz Yisrael*, the nations of the world will say, "Hashem is right to choose the Jews as His people, because they are a truthful people." But if the Jews will lie and cheat, the nations of the world will say, "What is this thing that Hashem has done? Why has He chosen to associate himself with thieves and liars?" Apparently, in the view of the Sma, the *geulah* will be delayed until the nations of the world will gladly attest to the honesty and integrity of the Jewish people.

All of us know full well where we have to improve.

We have to be honest with our employers. We have to deliver 60 minutes of honest work for every hour of pay. Our employers, for the most part, are not paying us to go to Minchah on their time. Our employers are not interested in providing us with free long-distance telephone time.

We have to be honest with our employees and give them everything to which they are entitled.

We have to be honest with the government. And if we perceive the government as being wasteful with our tax dollars, we are not exempt from being honest with the government. Which government was more corrupt than that of Czarist Russia? And yet, Rav Yaakov Kamenetsky, when he was a *rav* in Lithuania, always told people to make sure they gave the government every cent demanded by law.

We have to be honest with our schools and *shuls*. It is unconscionable to be less than absolutely truthful on a tuition-reduction form. It is beyond me how people can rationalize stealing from Torah institutions. It is beyond me how people make a large pledge during an appeal in *shul*, basking in all the admiring glances, and then neglect to pay up. What has become of us?

We have to be honest with ourselves. It is dishonest to pay lip service to the truth and then employ all sorts of clever subterfuges to avoid it. All the *shtick* and the gimmicks do not emanate from the realm of truth, and they are destructive to the soul.

But what are you supposed to do if everyone around you is bending the rules? What should you do if your competitors are milking the system for all its worth? Should you still deal fairly and honestly and allow them to gain the advantage over you?

The answer is yes, absolutely yes. Believe me, in the long run you will not lose out. Listen to this Midrash.

The Midrash relates that Falsehood came to Noach's Ark.

"Noach, I want to come along with you," said Falsehood. "I want to be in the new world."

"You can't come," said Noach, "because you need a partner. Only pairs are allowed onto the Ark. But you are not part of a pair. Get yourself a partner, and then we'll talk."

So Falsehood set in search of a partner, but who would be foolish enough to become partners with Falsehood? Finally, Falsehood managed to find a partner. It was Destruction.

"I'll make you a deal," Falsehood said to Destruction. "Let's go out and see what we can earn. Then we'll divide it equally between us."

And so this rather sordid pair, Falsehood and Destruction, made its way onto the Ark and were saved from the Flood.

A few thousand years later, Falsehood said to Destruction, "Let's make an accounting of everything we've earned. Where's all the profit we've made over the last few thousand years? It must be an astronomical number by now."

"Profit?" said Destruction. "Have you forgotten who your partner is? Don't you know my name? I'm Destruction. Anything I touch is destroyed. There is no profit, my friend. No profit at all."

That is the partnership that exists in the world today: Falsehood and Destruction; ill-gotten gains that will not last. They may last a month, a year, five years, but sooner or later, they will vanish. It may look like your competitors are gaining an unfair advantage by dishonest methods, but it is an illusion. Wherever Falsehood goes, Destruction cannot be far behind. They've been an inseparable pair for thousands of years.

Contemporary society is concerned with image rather than with substance. You drive the right car and wear the right clothes not because you want to do it but because you've got to project that image. Political candidates no longer stand for beliefs and convictions. They take polls to discover which way the wind is blowing and take positions upwind. And these positions shift from region to region. In one region, they project one image, and in another region they project another. But who are they really? Who is the person behind the image? Who knows?

All too many Jews project one image in the neighborhood and the *shtiebel* but take on an entirely different persona when they go to work downtown. All too many Jews keep vulgar language, ribald humor and a dash of flirtatiousness in their briefcases to be unpacked when they reach the office.

Rav Shamshon Raphael Hirsch once commented that some Jews have become reverse Marranos. The Marranos were gentiles on the outside but Jews on the inside. Some of us have become Jews on the outside but gentiles on the inside. The image is there, but with no substance behind it. Where is truth?

It's about time we stood up and told people who we really are. It may be a little hard at first. It may take special effort, but it will be well worth it — especially for the children. One thing most parents have in common is an obsession with bringing up good children. They read books, attend lectures, take courses, anything just to be a better parent. There is no magic formula to raising good children, but if anything comes close, it is honesty. Children who perceive their parents as honest, straightforward and sincere will be honest children, and honest children are good children. You cannot fool your children. If you are dishonest, they will know it and be dishonest themselves. But if you are honest, they too will be honest, and they will make you proud.

A man came to see a certain *rosh yeshivah* I know. "Let me ask you a question," he said. "Maybe you can explain it to me. I come from an old and very prestigious family. I am a learned man. I keep *glatt kosher* and do everything right, *lime-hadrin min hamedhadrin*. But I don't have any *nachas* from my children. My neighbor, on the other hand, is a simple person from a simple family. He keeps what he knows, which is not very much. And yet, each of his children is a gem. You know my neighbor, and you know me. How do you explain it?"

The *rosh yeshivah* looked at the man and said, "Are you prepared to hear something painful?"

"Yes, go ahead."

"You, my friend," said the *rosh yeshivah*, "are a refugee, a survivor. You came here with nothing and scraped and scratched until you were successful. If you had to bend the rules in order to get ahead, that was what you did. You could say one thing but mean another. That's what your children saw, that nothing really means anything. But your neighbor, that simple fellow, couldn't tell a lie if he tried. That's what his children saw. That's why they are what they are."

Rav Pam points out that being overly strict and overbearing with our children can cause them to lie. If they know they face terrible consequences if they are caught in a misdeed, they will be inclined to deny everything. And who could blame them? If you place undue emphasis on grades, they will be inclined to cheat on their exams. But having an honest child is far more important than having a child with good grades. If your child admits to having done something wrong and you punish him, you are in effect punishing him for his honesty. That is the worst message you can send.

Rav Pam learned about honesty from his mother who lived into her 90s. All his life, he never heard his mother say the word *sheker*, falsehood. She considered it a vulgar word and would not allow it to cross her lips. Instead, she would say, "It is not the truth," or, "He must be mistaken," but never, "It is a lie." That word was anathema to her. That is how to make an impression on a child. That is how to raise children like Rav Pam.

One final story.

One summer, my wife and I visited South Africa at the invitation of Ohr Somayach of South Africa. I am not sure if I was successful in inspiring them, but I myself was certainly inspired by the people I met.

It's a wonderful community organized around an Orthodox central *beis din*, whose authority is accepted by 90 percent of South African Jews, although they are not all observant. There is no Conservative presence, and hardly any Reform. Marriages, divorces, conversions and burials are all performed under the supervision of the *beis din* and are strictly kosher. These days, there is an unbelievable *ruach* of *teshuvah* in South Africa, and many hundreds of the non-observant are now becoming observant.

While I was there, I met many *roshei yeshivah* from *Eretz Yisrael* who came to South Africa to raise money. During one of his calls home, one *rosh yeshivah* was asked by his wife, "How are you doing?"

"Poorly," he replied.

"What's the matter?" she asked with sudden concern.

"Something's wrong with me," he said. "Everyone here is doing *teshuvah*. Except for me."

What's the secret of the vigorous movement towards *teshuvah* in South Africa? There are many theories. Some believe that the instability of the government causes people to seek out the rock-solid stability of the eternal Torah to anchor their lives. Others believe that the absence of television and the ban on obscenity for most of this century have allowed the people to remain moral and uncorrupted. Others give the credit to the Ponovezher Rav who had a special bond with the Jews of South Africa, most of whom are descended from Lithuanian Jews. The Ponovezher Rav used to beg them not to allow their children to marry out of the faith, no matter what. If the children remain Jewish, he insisted, the grandchildren will return. Whatever the reason, the Jewish community of South Africa is undergoing a veritable transformation.

About halfway through my stay, a woman called to ask me for an interview for a thesis she was writing about the *teshuvah* movement of South Africa.

"What can I tell you that you don't already know?" I asked her.

"Don't worry," she said. "Besides, I have a story I want to tell you."

The woman met with my wife and me, and we spoke about the movement for a while. I saw she really wanted to get to something else. Finally, she did.

"Let me tell you a story," she said. "Maybe you can tell me what it means."

"Go ahead," I said. "But I don't make any promises."

"Both my parents came to South Africa from Lithuania," she began. "My mother came from Ponovezh. My father had very little knowledge about anything Jewish, and he was completely non-observant. In fact, it fell to my mother to prepare my brothers for their *bar mitzvahs*.

"We lived in a small mining town, where my father had a store. He was an impeccably honest man. When the blacks, who were usually poor and illiterate, would come to sell their wares, my father always paid an honest price. His scales were scrupulously accurate. Other merchants in town would take advantage of the blacks by using inaccurate scales, but my father never cheated anyone.

"My father died many years ago and was buried in South Africa. My mother lived for 20 more years. She left instructions that when she died she was to be buried in *Eretz Yisrael* and that my father's body was also to be brought to Israel and buried next to her. She also asked that my son-in-law, who lives in *Eretz Yisrael*, should attend to the body. In accordance with her wishes, my father's casket was to be exhumed and sent to *Eretz Yisrael* for reburial.

"With my son-in-law looking on, the *chevra kadisha* in *Eretz Yisrael* donned masks over their mouths and noses before they opened the casket. The man had been dead for

20 years, and the stench of death would probably be over-powering. So they opened up the casket.

"*Shalem! Tzaddik!*" the man from the *chevra kadisha* shouted. *Shalem.* Intact. The body was perfectly intact. The deceased was clearly a *tzaddik.* My son-in-law peeked into the casket himself, and he confirms it. The body looked exactly like the picture of my father that sits on this mantelpiece."

The woman paused for a moment to gather her thoughts. "Rabbi, believe me," she said. "My father was no *tzaddik.* He was no righteous man. Believe me, I know. He was a good man, but not righteous. So what does this mean? How could his body still be intact after 20 years?"

I was as baffled as she was. How would I know the answer to such a question? All of a sudden, like a bolt of lightning from the sky, it hit me.

"Believe it or not," I said, "I think I may have an answer for you. There is a *passuk* in the Torah (*Devarim* 25:15) which states, '*Even shleimah vetzedek yihyeh lach.* You shall keep scales that are whole and righteous.' What did you tell me about your father? That he was honest, that he kept honest weights? Well, that was your father's reward. Since he kept scales that were *shalem*, he was *shalem*, intact. Since he kept scales that were *tzedek*, the *chevra kadisha* recognized him as a *tzaddik.* Hashem loves honest people."

The woman looked at me and started to cry. Then my wife started to cry. I have to admit that my eyes also became a little moist.

How powerful and wonderful is this thing called truth. It gives us meaning and direction throughout life. It nourishes our souls. It gives us good children. And it stands us in good stead long after we are gone from this world.

To Give
Is Divine

I WANT TO TELL YOU A STORY ABOUT A PERSON WHO WAS
famous for his selfless love for his fellow Jews. The story
takes place shortly before Pesach in Bucharest, Romania,
in the aftermath of the Holocaust. Refugees broken in spirit
and body are still streaming into the city from all directions,
hollow-eyed people intent on picking up the pieces of their
shattered lives. They will celebrate Pesach without the
warmth and comforts of home and hearth, but perhaps they
will have a piece of *matzah*, a glass of wine and some friend-
ly companionship.

In Bucharest at this time there is a great *tzaddik* known
as the Skulener Rebbe, a man thoroughly devoted to his
Jewish brethren. With Pesach approaching, he is busy bak-
ing *matzos* for distribution so that at least all the *rabbeim* and
rabbanim in the city can each have one *matzah*.

The Vizhnitzer Rebbe sends his son over.

"My father need two *matzos*," says the boy.

"Two *matzos*?" says the Skulener Rebbe. "How can I spare two *matzos* for him? I can barely give every *rebbe* one single *matzah*."

"My father said that he needs two *matzos*," the boy insists.

The Skulener Rebbe throws up his hands in defeat and gives the boy two *matzos*. "The Rebbe's wish is my command," he says.

Late in the afternoon on Erev Pesach, the Vizhnitzer Rebbe's son brings back one of the *matzos*.

"I don't understand," says the Skulener Rebbe. "I thought your father needed two *matzos*."

"He did," says the boy. "One for him, the other for you. He was afraid you would give away all the *matzos* and leave nothing for yourself. But now you will definitely have a *matzah*."

So who is the selfless person in this wonderful story?

It seems to me that there are two, the Skulener Rebbe who would give away his last *matzah* to another Jew and the Vizhnitzer Rebbe who is thoughtful enough to ensure that the Skulener Rebbe has *matzah* for Pesach. These are our *gedolim*, the people we admire and revere, the people we hold up as role models for our children and ourselves. They are the living embodiment of the holy Torah, the people who illuminate our world.

Now let us take a look at the other side of the picture, the dark side.

Living here in the United States of America at the end of the 20th century, we have to struggle mightily not to become totally self-absorbed and self-consumed. Never before has there been a society so saturated with wealth. Never before has there been a society in which ordinary people have been able to spend so much money on themselves. Never before has there been a society in which people have been bombarded with so many messages to buy, buy; consume, consume; indulge, indulge. The result is a society that reeks of selfishness.

If we go back just a few decades to the Seventies, we discover the beginnings of the contemporary outlook. "Do your own thing" was the battle cry of the Seventies. What does that mean? It means care about yourself, worry about yourself, and nothing and no one else.

Do your own thing. That's the slogan that worked its way into the very fabric of society and transformed America into what it is today. The institution of marriage has been ravaged, because marriage is all about sharing and not being focused on yourself. The birth rate has fallen to 2.3 children per family, because children are a hindrance to self-gratification. Were any of us with large families to walk into a supermarket with five or eight children, they would undoubtedly elicit nasty looks. Large families have no place in a selfish consumer society.

Two letters recently appeared in an etiquette advice column in a popular newspaper. A bride about to send out her wedding invitations wants to know if she may include a note asking the women not to wear white. A very serious problem apparently, because only the bride is allowed to be a vision in white. Or what about the weighty dilemma of the gentleman getting married in March? His sister wants to get married in January. Can he object "being that it's my year"? Now mind you, his sister is not asking, Heaven forbid, to get married during his *sheva berachos*. She wants to get married in January. But it's "my year."

These types of questions didn't arise 50 years ago. Not in Europe, not in America. There used to be a sense of higher purpose in society, but not anymore. Ours is a selfish, narcissistic generation. It is the Me Generation, uninterested in sacrifice, sharing or caring.

Contrast that with the Gemara in *Shabbos* (67a) which states that people should paint red stripes around the trunks of their trees that become sickly and stop producing fruit.

Passersby would understand that the tree was ailing, and they would pray for its recovery. This is the Jewish way. But would it work well in modern-day America? If you are having car problems and hang a red ribbon from your antenna, would passersby pray for its recovery? Highly unlikely.

So here we are, caught in the tug of war between two conflicting cultures. The time-honored Jewish way of life, based on the values and ideals of the Torah, calls for a transcendent selflessness, an abiding interest in the welfare of others. The modern American way of life is the exact opposite, totally self-centered, totally self-absorbed, totally selfish. So how do we live according to the Torah way despite the influences of the host society in which we find ourselves?

The first thing we have to realize is that selfishness is essentially a form of *avodah zarah*, idol worship. Selfishness is really self-worship. The Psalmist tells us (*Tehillim* 81:10), "You shall have no alien gods among you." Our Sages (*Shabbos* 105b) comment, "Which alien gods dwell among you? The evil inclination which is within each person." Within each and every one of us there is an alien god called *Anochi*, self, and our entire lifetime is one long struggle to resist the worship of this god.

If you think about it, the greatest impediment between us and Hashem is the *Anochi*, the self. Moshe Rabbeinu tells the Jewish people (*Devarim* 5:5), "*Anochi omeid bein Hashem uveineichem*. I am standing between Hashem and you." The Baal Shem Tov, in a classic Chassidic interpretation, read the *passuk* as saying, "The *Anochi* stands between Hashem and you." That alien god called *Anochi*, the worship of the self, the ego, that is what stands between you and Hashem. That is the great divide.

We must decide once and for all who stands at the center of our universe. Is it Hashem? Or is it the great Me, the alien god otherwise known as *Anochi*?

Every issue of *bein adam laMakom*, our relationship with Hashem, always comes down to this question. Should we or should we not get up for *minyan*? Should we or should we not make an extra effort to learn even though we are tired? The question is essentially whether we should sacrifice our comfort and convenience in order to fulfill our obligation to Hashem. In other words, who has priority, Hashem or us?

If we think a little more deeply into it, it also becomes apparent that every single issue of *bein adam lachaveiro*, our relationships with other people, also hinges on the exact same question. Who is at the center of our universe, Hashem or us? Think about it. Every argument we get into, every domestic squabble, aren't they all motivated by our overbearing egos? Aren't we always motivated by our perceived needs and rights? Who should choose the baby's name, you or I? Should we go to your parents for Pesach or mine? Do we keep the air conditioner on or do we shut it off? It is always in defense of our turf, of our needs and wants, of our rights. It is defense of the alien god named *Anochi*.

So what do we do about it? Can we solve the problem by a conscious resolution to be selfless? Unfortunately, it is not so simple.

We can resolve to stop talking *lashon hara*, we can actually stop in our tracks if we make a great effort, because people were not created with a fundamental need to speak *lashon hara*. We can resolve to speak only the truth, because people were not created with a fundamental need to cheat and lie. But we cannot simply resolve to stop loving ourselves, to stop caring about ourselves, to stop worrying about ourselves, because the sense of self is part of our fundamental nature.

Ahavas atzmo, the love of self, is part and parcel of the human condition. Hashem created every single human being with a love of self, because it would be impossible to function without it. A person must recognize that he is a somebody, that he has intrinsic worth, before he can be expected to accomplish anything at all. A person serves Hashem because "I want to do it." There must be an "I" who is motivated and energized. If not, why should he make the effort?

The Torah gives us a *mitzvah* called *ve'ahavta lerei'acha kamocha*, you shall love others as you love yourself. Rav Eliahu Dessler points out that this is a tacit endorsement of the love of self. Otherwise, how could the Torah command us to love others as ourselves, if we are in fact not supposed to love ourselves?

Rav Dessler goes on to write about a young woman whose husband was deathly ill. One night, the woman dreamed that her husband had died. The first thoughts that came into her mind were about her own needs. What's going to be with me? Where should I live? Should I live by myself or return to my parents? How will I care for the children?

A week later her husband died, and she was overcome with guilt.

"I am a terrible wife," she told Rav Dessler. "What kind of *teshuvah* should I do? Here my husband is about to die, and what am I worried about? I'm worried about where I should live. My husband's dying and I'm worried about me. What kind of wife am I?"

"You bear no blame whatsoever," Rav Dessler said to her. "Because your dream only revealed the truth to you. Yes, the truth. Your sense of self-preservation is stronger than the love you had for your husband. There is nothing to be ashamed of. You had a good marriage. You were a good wife. But that is human nature. People think first about themselves."

So we are faced with an anomaly. On the one hand, we need a certain degree of *ahavas atzmo*, a love and concern for ourselves, in order to exist. On the other hand, that love and caring for ourselves can distort and corrupt our lives. Herein lies one of the most basic challenges of life. How do we prevent self-love from becoming self-worship? How do we avoid becoming so preoccupied with ourselves that we forget about everything and everybody else? How do we achieve a proper balance?

One of the most effective ways to overcome selfishness is by getting involved in projects that are focused on the needs of others. Spending serious volunteer time working for a *kiruv* organization, a *bikur cholim* or a charity is an excellent option. People who are married and have children, however, do not have to go far afield to find opportunities for selflessness.

Marriage is not about finding a spouse who will take the place of a mother or father and provide the care to which we have become accustomed in childhood. Marriage is not about taking. It is about sharing and giving and caring. Marriage is about learning how to say "we" instead of "I," to think in terms of "us" rather than "me." Marriage is one of the paths that lead us out of the shell of selfishness. Indeed, the Gemara (*Yevamos* 63a) states that "whoever lacks a wife is not a complete person."

There is also another way to break out of the shell of selfishness, and that is by having children. Children are about giving. Children are about waking up at 2 o'clock in the morning because they're hungry and changing their diapers when they are wet and feeding them again and rocking them to sleep. And that is just the beginning. Children are about giving and giving and giving and giving some more.

Rav Moshe Shapiro, speaking at a meeting of TAFKID, a New York organization of parents of severely handicapped children, told an interesting story about a young *talmid chacham* in Yerushalayim who had a large family. One day, an uncle came into his house and saw him surrounded by little children. He was holding a child on each knee, and several more were on both sides of him. The young man, however, was unperturbed. He listened and spoke patiently to each of the children.

"I want to ask you a question," said the uncle. "How will your children ever repay you for what you have done for them?"

The young man thought about the question for a while. "A good question," he said. "You know what I think? You know how they'll repay me? By giving me a measure of immortality, by carrying my name forward. They will take my place and their children after them for generation after generation for all time. That is what they will give me."

A short while afterwards, the young man went to see the Brisker Rav and decided to ask him what he thought of his uncle's question and his own response.

The Brisker Rav shook his head in disapproval. "The answer you gave is close to blasphemy. Children have nothing to do with repayment. They are not an investment for future *nachas*. You can pray for *nachas*, just like you pray for health and prosperity, but that is not why you have children. Children are about giving. It's the way Hashem wants us to emulate His ways.

"Let me ask you, why did Hashem create us? For the *nachas* he expected to get from us? Does He really have a lot of *nachas* from us? Well, I'm telling you He doesn't have much *nachas* from us. He created us because He loves to do good, because He loves to give. And that's why we have to have children — to emulate Hashem's ways, to give."

In light of this story, Rav Moshe Shapiro spoke words of encouragement to the assembled parents of severely handicapped children. "You have a special *zchus*," he told them. "You are true parents. When we say in Selichos, *kerachem av al banim*, asking Hashem to have mercy on us as a father has mercy on his children, we are speaking of parents such as you. You give to your children without the expectation of conventional *nachas,* but you give anyway. You have compassion for your children. You have patience with your children. You expect nothing in return, and yet, you give without measure. You are true parents."

There is a common saying that to err is human, to forgive is Divine. I would like to paraphrase that: To take is human, to give is Divine.

Marriage and children. These are the bridges by which we cross from our insular world into the world of others.

That explains why the Torah required the *Kohen Gadol*, who performed the *Avodah* on Yom Kippur, to have a wife on Yom Kippur. What other position in Jewish life requires that the appointee be married? A judge has to have children, but he doesn't have to be married while he presides over his court. Why then must a *Kohen Gadol* be married in order to serve on Yom Kippur?

It is essential to the *Kohen* Gadol's role, explains Rav Kook, because on Yom Kippur he must secure forgiveness for all the Jewish people. If he bears the hopes and aspirations of *Klal Yisrael* on his shoulders, he cannot be self-absorbed and self-centered. He cannot be wrapped up in himself. Therefore, he must be married. He has to be accustomed to living not only for himself but for others as well. Moreover, even though he is married, he must be separated from his home for seven days before Yom Kippur. Why? So that he will expand his focus beyond his wife and children to include the broader community of *Klal Yisrael*.

Perhaps that is why he is called the *Kohen Gadol*, the Great *Kohen*. Why wasn't he called the *Kohen Rishon*, the First *Kohen*, just as the leading ministers are called Prime Ministers or First Ministers? Perhaps it is because the word *gadol*, great, connotes a person who is bigger than himself. The Torah tells us (*Shemos* 2:11), "*Vayigdal Moshe*. And Moshe reached adulthood." But it can also be read, "And Moshe became a *gadol*, a great person." How did he become a *gadol*? Let us read on. "*Vayeitzei el echav vayar besivlosam*. And he went out among his brothers and he saw their drudgery." What made Moshe Rabbeinu into a *gadol*? He didn't stay in the lap of luxury in the palace of Pharaoh. He became a *gadol* because he went out among his brothers and shared in their agony. That's a *gadol*, a person that thinks about others. That was the *Kohen Gadol*.

Think about it. We always talk about *gedolim*. Everybody

has a conception of what constitutes a *gadol*: someone who is full of Torah; someone who is full of *yiras Shamayim*. Of course, these are correct. But a *gadol* is more than that. He is someone who is dedicated to the community. That is the path to Jewish greatness, getting out of the narrow confines of the selfish world and stepping into the world of others.

There's a famous story about the Baal HaTanya, the founder of the Lubavitcher dynasty, which took place while he was a *talmid* in the *beis midrash* of the Maggid of Mezritch.

One evening, he knocked on the Maggid's door.

"Who is there?" asked the Maggid.

"*Ich*," said the Baal HaTanya. "It is I."

No answer.

He knocked again.

"Who is there?" asked the Maggid again.

"*Ich*," said the Baal HaTanya again. "It is I."

Again no answer.

He knocked a third time.

"Who is there?" asked the Maggid.

This time the Baal HaTanya said, "Zalman."

The Maggid let him in.

"Listen to me," said the Maggid. "Tomorrow, there is a *bris* in the city. I want you to go there and join them for the *seudah*."

The Baal HaTanya was puzzled, but he obeyed without question. The next day, he took a seat at the *seudah* and began to eat.

All of a sudden, the waiter pointed at him and shouted, "Thief! He is the one who stole the silverware. It's him, the one sitting at the end of the table."

The Baal HaTanya was dismayed. "*Nisht ich, nisht ich*," he protested. "It's not me. It's not me."

This was what the Maggid wanted to impress on the Baal HaTanya. If he was to be a leader of the Jewish people, he needed to rise above the *ich*, the ego. He needed to cry, *"Nisht ich!"* He needed to negate the ego and focus his thoughts on others. To be a *gadol* you have to think about others.

I recently read a story about Rav Gedaliah Moshe Goldman, the Rebbe of Zhivil. After spending seven and a half years in a labor camp in Siberia, he and another Jewish prisoner, an elderly man, were summoned to the Commandant's office.

"You can leave," said the Commandant. "You are free to leave. All you have to do is sign the paper."

But it was Shabbos. What was he supposed to do?

Thus began an internal debate.

Can I sign the paper? It's Shabbos. How can I sign the paper on Shabbos?

Of course, I can sign. It's *pikuach nefesh*, a matter of life and death.

But is it really a matter of life and death? So I'll stay here for another six months, another year, another two years, is that so terrible? I survived until now. I can stay longer. Is it really a matter of life and death? So I'll stay here.

"I'm not signing the paper," he told the Commandant.

"You're not signing the paper?" he said. "Suit yourself. So you'll sit. As far as I'm concerned, you can sit here forever."

He turned to the other prisoner. "Sign," he said, "and you're free."

"I can't sign," said the other prisoner. "It's Shabbos."

The Rebbe of Zhivil jumped up. "Wait a minute," he cried. "I'll sign for him. You can set him free."

"I don't understand," said the Commandant. "A moment ago you told me you can't sign. And now you're offering to sign for him?"

"I cannot sign for myself," said the Rebbe of Zhivil, "because I am not sure that this is a matter of life and death for me. But the other prisoner is an old man. He will not survive if he stays in this place. For him I can definitely sign."

The Commandant was awed by what he had just heard. "You were willing to remain here because you couldn't sign," he said, "and you are prepared to sign for someone else. I am impressed. You both can go."

Impressive indeed. That's a *gadol*.

There is an old Yiddish saying which declares that a baby comes into this world with its hands clenched into little fists. Every baby comes into this world wanting it all. He is interested only in himself. He wakes up at night and cries out to be fed, with no regard for the comfort of his parents. That's a baby: self-consumed; wanting to grab it all in his little fists.

So what *berachah* do we give this little baby at the *bris*? "*Zeh hakatan gadol yihyeh.* Let this little one become big." Let this baby, whose smallness is expressed in his selfishness, become a *gadol*. Let him become great, not only in Torah, not only in *yiras Shamayim*. That may not always be feasible for some of us. But everyone can aspire to becoming a *gadol* in the sense that he cares about others, that he can get beyond his own selfish narrow world.

Twenty-five years ago, I had the privilege of making the acquaintance of a very special man from Bnei Brak named Reb Herschel. He was visiting Baltimore at the time, and I have kept in touch with him ever since. Reb Herschel is not a famous *rav* or *rosh yeshivah,* but he is the epitome of an *ehrlicher Yid.* That phrase doesn't translate well into English, but I guess we could say it means an upstanding Jew.

On the day he commemorated the *yahrzeit* of his father, Reb Herschel found himself in a *shul* in a different neighborhood of Bnei Brak. He asked if he could take the *amud*, and it was given to him. A friend of his happened to be in the *shul* at the time, and being accustomed to Reb Herschel's passionate *tefillos*, he prepared himself for an unexpected treat. Now, we're going to have a real *tefillah*, he thought. But Reb Herschel let him down. He went to the *amud*, and before you could turn around, he was finished.

"Reb Herschel, what came over you?" his friend complained to him afterwards. "Where was your passion, your fire? I was expecting so much, and I was disappointed."

"Don't be upset," said Reb Herschel. "There was really nothing I could do. I looked at the faces of the people, and I could see exactly what they were thinking. *Oy vey*, look who's at the *amud*. It looks like we're going to be here forever. So tell me, my friend, what could I do? I'm supposed to be the *shliach tzibbur*, the representative of the people. I have to do what they want. Do you know what they want? They want to go to work. They want to finish with the *tefillah* and leave. They aren't interested in my passionate and fiery *tefillos*, so I have no right."

How many people would think this way? How many times have we seen people stretch out the *tefillah*, no matter where they are? But not Reb Herschel. His first thought was of the sensitivities of other people. That's a *gadol*.

So how do we become like that? So many of us are married and have children and are still selfish. We still care about and worry about ourselves and not about other people. The answer, as always, is to begin with the small things, to make small changes and take small steps until we effect a major turnaround. What we do influences what we are, so that if we consciously choose to act a certain way it will eventually become our nature. We form a new mindset.

In fact, it is important that we start only with small things. If we suddenly decide to become instantly selfless by having 25 people for Shabbos and staying up until 3 o'clock in the morning to wash the dishes, it might last for one week — certainly not longer. And then everything goes back to the way it was, and selflessness is forgotten. It has to happen in small steps so that it becomes natural and comfortable, so that it becomes what you are rather than what you do.

Try complimenting people. That's not such a difficult thing to do. It's a doable small step. How much does it cost to compliment somebody? Someone *davens* nicely for the *amud*, tell him you enjoyed it. A woman who meets someone she knows can tell her she looks beautiful. She can compliment her *sheitel*. What does it cost you? What does it cost you to say a nice word?

What does it cost every once in a while to call up your child's teacher or *rebbi* and tell him how happy your child is? What does it cost to call up the principal and compliment him on his work? We're always there to complain when things go wrong. Why can't we be there to give compliments when they go well?

Start giving compliments. If you can't be generous with your money or your time or your energies, at least be generous with your words. We all know how to do that.

Sometimes when I come to my *shiur* room, there are not enough chairs for all the *bachurim*, and they have to go to other classrooms to bring more chairs. I always tell them what Rav Shraga Feivel Mendlowitz would say in a similar situation if a *bachur* came back with a single chair, "You bring one chair, you're a *shlepper*. You bring two chairs, you're a *baal chessed*."

One chair means you thought only about yourself. Two chairs means you thought about others as well. Is it really so hard to bring two chairs? They're not heavy for these vigorous young men. So why bring only one? Because you are not accustomed to thinking about others. The answer, therefore, is to become accustomed. Train yourself to bring two chairs, and before you know it, you will indeed be thinking about others. You will become conditioned to it. It will become part of your nature, your mindset.

Here's another situation where you can make a difference without much effort. A *meshulach* is circulating around the *shul* with his plastic-covered letter of recommendation. If you're only going to give him a dollar, there's no reason to take five minutes to scrutinize the letter. And when you give that dollar, give it with a smile. Some people don't even look the *meshulach* in the face. How does it make him feel?

It's not very pleasant to be a *meshulach*, to go from place to place begging for dollars. At least, you can shine a little sunlight into his life. All it takes is a smile. Give him a dollar, and you're a *baal tzedakah*. Give it with a smile, and you're also a *baal chessed*. It shows you thought about him as a human being.

A real estate agent in Baltimore, Maryland, told me, "You know, I take people around to look for homes. One month, two months, three months, and nothing comes up. They don't like anything. Finally, after three months, I show them a house they like. I take them home, and what do they do right away? They call the owner to find out when the listing expires so that they can wait it out and buy it without paying me a commission. Is this right?"

How indeed can people do these things? Where is simple *mentchlichkeit*? A person spends a month of Sundays taking them around to house after house, and then when it comes time to close the deal, they cheat him out of his commission? For what? For a few thousand dollars? For the cost of that Jacuzzi they intend to install after they buy the house? How can people do such things?

There is only one answer: Selfishness. To these people, no one else exists in the world besides them. They never think of the other person, only themselves. It does not enter their mind that they've imposed on a man who is trying to make a living to support his family. They just grab what they can to feed their own needs and desires, never thinking about who gets trampled in the process.

So why don't people make the effort to become more selfless? It is because they're afraid. They're afraid that if they become selfless and giving, the worst thing will happen. They won't be happy. They'll be so busy giving to others and worrying about them that they won't be able to enjoy.

Ironically, however, the exact opposite is true. The more you give, the less self-absorbed you are, the less things bother you, and the happier you become. The self-centered person believes that the world owes him, that everything has to go his way, and therefore, he is constantly unhappy, constantly upset that things aren't going his way. But the selfless person is not concerned about himself, and he is at peace with the world. Nothing bothers him, and he is supremely happy. That's the irony.

The Mishnah says in *Avos*, "*Omdin tzefufin umishtachavim lirevachah.* [In the *Beis Hamikdash*,] people stood crowded together, but when they bowed down there was ample space for all." I once heard an interpretation of these words. When you stand up for your rights, you always feel crowded, but when you bow down, when you're willing to bend and to give, you find you have ample space.

We know that selflessness makes a person better and happier. But it goes even further than that. It makes him safer. In Heaven, the selfish person and the selfless person are measured on two different scales.

The Gemara (*Rosh Hashanah* 17a) tells us, "*Kal hamaavir al midosav maavirin lo al pesha'av.* If a person is willing to forgo his rights, Hashem is willing to remove his sins." The selfish person must pay for his sins, but the selfless person goes free.

How does this work? Why is there a double standard?

Rav Chaim Friedlander, in the *Sifsei Chaim*, explains at length. He establishes that sin is destructive because it distances the sinner from Hashem. *Teshuvah* expiates sin because it brings the sinner closer to Hashem. *Teshuvah* is return, closing the distance and drawing near. Unless a person does *teshuvah*, he must be punished in order to obliterate the sin and remove the impediment to closeness with Hashem.

But there is also another way to draw near to Hashem. A person who emulates the ways of Hashem by rising above selfish concerns and focusing on the needs of others is naturally closer to Hashem. Therefore, a person who is selfless can avoid punishment for his sins.

In the beginning of *Sefer Yehoshua,* we read about Rachav, who had been a woman of ill repute for 40 years. Eventually, she married Yehoshua bin Nun, the leader of the Jewish people, and she became the ancestress of 8 Jewish prophets.

The Alter of Kelm finds this incredible. How does a woman jettison 40 years of sinfulness, 40 years of promiscuity, 40 years of decadence, and just turn it all around and marry the great leader of the Jewish people?

It was an act of selflessness, explains the Alter of Kelm, plain and simple. She was willing to risk her life for the two spies. She took them in and hid them on pain of death. That one act of selflessness obliterated the wall that had risen during those numerous years of sinfulness. That one act of selflessness brought her closer to Hashem.

Let me conclude with the following stories about the Klausenberger Rebbe, which took place shortly after the war.

It was Erev Yom Kippur in the displaced persons camps in Germany. As the sun began its long descent into the western sky, the Klausenberger Rebbe began the elaborate spiritual and mystical preparations which *Chassidishe rebbes* are accustomed to making at such auspicious times. After all, how could a person possibly expect to stand before the Almighty on the holiest day of the year without extensive preparation and introspection? From the vague edges of his consciousness, he heard a muffled knock. Pulling himself back into the mundane world, he realized there was someone at the door.

It was a young girl, one of the residents of the camp.

"I want to ask a favor," she said. "My father used to give me his blessing every Erev Yom Kippur. But I don't have a father anymore." She suppressed a sob and continued. "Can the Rebbe bless me instead?"

"Of course, my child," said the Rebbe. He placed his hands above her head, shut his eyes in concentration and recited the blessing.

The girl left with a happy smile on her face, and the Rebbe returned to his preparations. Five minutes later, he was again interrupted by a knock on the door. Another girl wanted a favor. She, too, had lost her father and wanted the Rebbe to give her his blessing.

"Of course, my child," said the Rebbe. He blessed her and returned to his preparations.

Eighty-seven times that day there was a knock on the door. Eighty-seven times that day a forlorn young survivor appeared at his door. Eighty-seven times that day the Rebbe recited the parental blessing over an orphaned head. The Rebbe never did get back to his customary preparations on that Erev Yom Kippur in the displaced persons camps. His preparations that year were of an altogether different and far more exalted nature. He came before the Almighty having gladdened the hearts and brightened the eyes of 87 orphans.

On another occasion, the Klausenberger Rebbe noticed that a young girl in the camp was not wearing socks.

"My dear child," he said to her kindly, "a Jewish girl does not go about without socks."

"Rebbe, I don't even have enough bread to eat," the girl said to him. "How do you expect me to have socks?"

The Rebbe nodded gravely. "You are right," he said.

He sat down on the ground and removed his shoes. Then he took off his socks and handed them to her.

"Now you have socks," he said.

This story was not known until the Rebbe passed away in Yerushalayim nearly 50 years later. During the *shivah*, a woman came in carrying a paper bag. She told the family what had happened that day in the camps, then she opened the bag and pulled out a pair of socks. "These are the socks he gave me off his own feet," she said. "They are my most treasured possessions."

On yet another occasion, a young man came to see the Rebbe at the insistence of his friends. The young man had been a sincere, religious boy. He survived the nightmare of the concentration camps, but the rest of his family did not. Now he was bitter and angry. Gone were the *tefillin* and the *tzitzis*. Gone were the *yarmulke* and the *sefarim*. He wanted nothing to do with anything religious.

"What happened to you?" his friends wanted to know when they met him after the war.

"I've had enough," he replied. "Hashem took the good and left only the debris. He took my whole family, everyone that was good, and He left only me. Well, I have had enough."

No amount of arguing or cajoling could budge him, until one fellow had a bright idea. "Go and see the Klausenberger Rebbe," he said. "At least, listen to what he has to say before you throw everything away."

The young man reluctantly agreed to see the Rebbe.

The Rebbe took one look at him and saw immediately what was going on with the young man. "What is in your heart?" he asked.

"Hashem took the good," the young man replied, "and left only the debris. He took my whole family and left only me."

The Rebbe looked at him, and his eyes filled with tears. "It's true," he said. "It is so true. Hashem took my wife and my 11 children. And He left only me. He took away the good, and He left the debris."

For the next 20 minutes, the Rebbe and the young man sat together and cried.

The young man did indeed come back to Torah and *Yiddishkeit*. Years later, he used to say, "If the Rebbe had given me one word of rebuke I would have walked out and never come back. But the Rebbe didn't rebuke me. The Rebbe cried with me."

When I reflect on the greatness of the Klausenberger Rebbe which shines forth from these poignant stories, I often wonder if we ourselves could aspire to such greatness. Could we devote our entire Erev Yom Kippur to blessing orphaned children? We probably could do that. Would we take the socks off our feet and give them to a destitute girl? Perhaps. But could we cry with a broken-hearted young man? That is a challenging question.

The Rebbe could do it because he had achieved greatness by rising above the narrowness of his own self. He was not wrapped up in his own needs and his own desires. He was undoubtedly the one who always made sure that others had chairs. He was undoubtedly the one who always thought about other people before himself, who praised others and made them feel good about themselves.

That is how we become people who would give someone the socks off our own feet. That is how we become people who can cry from the pain that is in someone else's heart.

Let My Name Be Sanctified

W HEN THE NAZIS ROSE TO POWER IN GERMANY IN 1933, Rav Shimon Schwab was a young *rav* in Bavaria. It was a terrible time, a time of tremendous uncertainties. Jews were arrested on the slightest pretext, imprisoned and often executed. Heaven help the Jew who fell into the hands of the Gestapo.

One Shabbos, Rav Schwab was speaking about the sin of the *eigel* (Golden Calf). The sin of the Jewish people, he explained, was not outright idolatry. They looked to the *eigel* as an intermediary, a *vermittler* in German, between humankind and Hashem. "But we can speak directly to Hashem," he concluded. "We don't need a *vermittler*."

One of the people mistakenly thought that Rav Schwab had said, "We don't need a Hitler." This pathetic Jew, hoping to curry favor with the new powers that be, immediately ran to the Gestapo to report that the rabbi had made subversive statements.

The Gestapo summoned Rav Schwab and accused him of sedition. Rav Schwab explained that it was all a mistake. He used his *Hirsch Chumash* to demonstrate what he had actually said to corroborate his defense.

"There," he said, pointing to the passage he had quoted. "There's the word I said. *Vermittler*, not Hitler."

It seemed fairly open and shut, a simple misunderstanding, but nothing was ever simple with the Gestapo, even in the very early days. Once they got a rabbi into their clutches, they did not let him off so easily. Rav Schwab spent two full months waiting to hear what his fate would be.

During those two bone-chilling months, Rav Schwab slept in his clothes every night. Why? Because he did not know from one moment to the next if he might be taken out to the gallows and hanged. He had heard that the Gestapo liked to pull people from their beds in the middle of the night and hang them from the gallows in their nightclothes. It was a very effective way of humiliating the victim and intimidating everyone else. "But I am a *rav*," Rabbi Schwab later explained. "It would have been a *chillul Hashem* for a *rav* to be hanged improperly dressed." Therefore, for two whole months Rav Schwab never took off his clothes.

Imagine. Here is a man who, from one moment to the next, doesn't know if he will live or die, and what does he worry about? He is worried about a *chillul Hashem* should he be hanged in his nightclothes. His foremost thought was not his own survival but the sanctity of Hashem's Name.

Going back a bit into history, we find a precedent for this story. The Torah tells us that when Lot was taken prisoner, in the War of the Four Kings, Og came running to tell Avraham all about it. In this context, the Torah refers to Avraham as *Avraham Halvri*. Nowhere else in the Torah is Avraham called *Avraham Halvri*. Why?

Rav Dov Weinberger explains that Og was actually sending Avraham on a suicide mission. After all, how could Avraham be victorious against the four most powerful kings of Mesopotamia? But if so, why indeed did Avraham under-take a rescue mission against impossible odds? What com-pelled him to do such a thing? What motivated him?

The answer is: *Avraham Halvri.* Our Sages tell us that he was called Ivri because "*kol haolam kulo omeid betzad echad vehu me'ever hasheini.*" The entire world could be aligned on one side, and he would not hesitate to align him-self on the other side if that was where his convictions lay. He would stop at nothing to defend his beliefs and convictions.

When Avraham heard that Lot had been taken captive, he realized that the honor of Hashem was in great danger. Avraham and his nephew Lot could easily have passed for identical twins so similar were they in appearance. Therefore, Avraham was afraid that the victorious kings would claim that they had captured him rather than his nephew. "Where is your Creator now?" they would say as they paraded him through the streets. And Hashem's Name would be desecrated. And so with no thought for his own safety and the hopelessness of his mission, Avraham set off in pursuit of Lot's captors. It was unthinkable for him to stand by and allow a *chillul Hashem* to take place if there was any-thing he could do to prevent it.

The Rambam in *Hilchos Yesodei Hatorah* (5:11) writes that *chillul Hashem* does not necessarily derive from a vio-lation of the Torah. If a *talmid chacham* performs any act that results in a negative public reaction it is considered a *chillul Hashem.*

The Chafetz Chaim once saw his son about to do some-thing.

"Be very careful," said the Chafetz Chaim. "If a *talmid chacham* were to do such a thing unsuccessfully, it would result in a *chillul Hashem.*"

The Chafetz Chaim's son smiled. "You wouldn't exactly call me a *talmid chacham*, would you?"

"You are enough of a *talmid chacham*," the Chafetz Chaim replied, "to be obligated to prevent a *chillul Hashem.*" In other words, if a person is considered a *talmid chacham* in the public perception, he has all the obligations of a *talmid chacham* with regard to the prevention of a *chillul Hashem*. Any negative public reaction he causes would be considered a *chillul Hashem*, even if he did not violate a single letter in the Torah.

In today's day and age, I believe, this broad definition of a *talmid chacham* would be expanded even further. Indeed, any demonstrably observant Jew bears the full obligations of a *talmid chacham*. Gentile and secular Jews do not differentiate among Orthodox Jews. In their eyes, we are all rabbis, and therefore, we all have the obligations of rabbis. We are all ambassadors of the Torah. To them, we all personify the Torah, and we must therefore act accordingly.

If so, we must measure everything we do and say by the most stringent standards of *chillul Hashem*. How do we talk? What kind of language do we use? Is it befitting a rabbi? How do we drive through the streets? Are we aggressive? Do we cut into every break in the traffic? The *Shulchan Aruch* does not establish rules for driving in traffic, but are we making a *chillul Hashem*? People see an observant Jew, and they immediately think, Rabbi! Are we helping them form a positive image of a rabbi, the embodiment of Torah?

What we do and don't do will shape people's image of Torah. And we must ask ourselves some hard questions. Are we good ambassadors? What image comes to mind when people think about Orthodox Jews?

The Gemara (Yoma 86a) tells us to be gentle in our relations with other people. About one who acts in this manner it will be said, "Fortunate is his father who taught him Torah. Fortunate is his teacher who taught him Torah. How beautiful are his deeds! How admirable are his ways!"

Is that what people think when they encounter a typical Orthodox Jew?

A little while ago, while I was traveling on a plane, I saw that there was another observant Jew among the passengers. As the plane prepared to land, the flight attendant made the announcement we all know by heart, "Passengers, please remain seated until the plane comes to a complete stop and the pilot has turned off the 'fasten seat belt' sign."

As often happens in big city airports, the plane was delayed on the runway, and the seat belt sign remained on for much longer than expected. So did the people follow instructions and remain in their seats or not? All of us remained seated, except for one man. I'm sure you can guess who it was (and it wasn't me). That's right. While the plane was still taxiing on the runway, this highly recognizable observant Jew stood up and started getting his things together. I didn't watch him, but I did watch the faces of the other passengers. Believe me, it was a real *chillul Hashem*. In their eyes, this man represented the Torah, and he brought it dishonor.

I once heard something very disturbing. I don't know if it is true or not, but if such a story is even making the rounds something is dreadfully wrong. They say that a Tower airplane once landed in *Eretz Yisrael* towards the end of December. About half the passengers were Jews and the other half were Christian Yuletide travelers. This plane was also delayed on the runway, and by the time it reached the terminal, many passengers were pulling their carry-on luggage from the overhead bins. The stewardess got on the public address system and said, "To all of you who are standing, we want to wish you a Happy Chanukah and to all those seated, we wish you Seasons Greetings."

Obviously, there's a perception out in the world that there's something out of line with Orthodox Jews. What do people think of us? That we're rude and grasping? What a horrendous *chillul Hashem*!

We each have the responsibility to accomplish the exact opposite. We have to live a life of *kiddush Hashem*, of sanctity and transcendence. We have to implant in people's minds that Orthodox Jews are people of exceptional virtue and decorum. We have to persuade people to admire us and, by extension, to admire the Torah.

There is a tendency to think that people have many different jobs. Some of us are professionals, some are businesspeople. Some are employers, some are employees. But that is really a mistaken perception. We do not have different jobs. We have different means of earning a living, but we all have the same job. It is the first and foremost job of each and every one of us to promote *kiddush Hashem*, to bring glory and honor to His Name.

It is all a question of priorities. If you think your job is to be a doctor or a lawyer or a businessperson or a teacher, your decisions will be geared to the furtherance of your career or your business. But if you recognize that your job is really to make a *kiddush Hashem*, then that will always be your first consideration in any situation that arises.

Some years ago, there was a terrible fire in Massachusetts, and a large textile mill called Malden Mills burned to the ground. The owner of Malden Mills is an Orthodox Jew named Aaron Feuerstein, whose father was the founding president of Torah Umesorah.

Mr. Feuerstein could easily have taken the insurance money and lived in luxury for the rest of his life. Instead, he did something very remarkable and noble. He decided to rebuild, and while the plant was being rebuilt, he kept all his employees on the payroll. It was such a stunning move that it captured the imagination of the American people. No matter where you turned, you could not help but hear about this Orthodox Jew named Aaron Feuerstein. It was on the front pages of all the papers, and it was written up as a feature article in the *Reader's Digest*. Hundreds of millions of people read about Mr. Feuerstein's decision.

What was that decision based on? Was it purely business? Was it good for the bottom line to keep idle workers on the payroll for close to a year and keep their health insurance going? Or was it just the right thing to do?

It was an ethical thing to do, and I like to believe that Mr. Feuerstein intended to make a spectacular *kiddush Hashem*.

But it is not enough for the occasional individual to make a *kiddush Hashem*. Each of us must make a *kiddush Hashem* so that the world at large will become convinced that lofty Jewish standards are not restricted to a few isolated individuals. We need to show the world that high-mindedness is what our community is all about. And we can do it.

Not long ago, *The New York Times* published an article entitled *"Status in America."* The article explored the criteria of status in the vast mosaic of subcultures that make up American society. What sorts of accomplishments confer status in different segments of society? The answers were illuminating.

Take truck drivers in America. What gives a truck driver status? The answer is, to have driven three million miles without so much as a fender bender. Now that is status.

What's status for a fighter pilot? It's not enough to fly an F-14 and land it safely on an aircraft carrier in the middle of the night on a storm-tossed sea. You also have to have shot down an enemy aircraft in a real dogfight.

And how about Orthodox Jews? What is considered status among Orthodox Jews? The answer is, according to *The New York Times*:"Studying, Studying and More Studying." The article then proceeds to interview a young man from the Chaim Berlin Kollel. "Our ideal of greatness," he is quoted as saying, "is defined by forgoing materialism in the pursuit of scholarship. This is our status symbol."

It seems obvious, the reporter from the *Times* comments, that in Orthodox Jewish society it is not the doctor who inspires admiration but the *dayan* (Rabbinic judge). A lawyer is less impressive than a scholar. It is a pity that the languishing graduate student in the secular world doesn't share this ethic of learning for learning's sake.

Apparently, enough of us have been making a *kiddush Hashem* to capture the attention of *The New York Times*. But we have to do more, much more. That perception has to spread to the farthest corners of society until every person in the street will know that we are a holy people.

The *mitzvah* of *kiddush Hashem* is expressed in the Torah as "*Venikdashti besoch bnei Yisrael*, and My Name shall become sanctified among the people of Israel." Why, ask the commentators, is it expressed in the reflexive form, "shall become sanctified"? Why doesn't the Torah command us outright, "*Tekadshu es shemi*, sanctify My Name"?

Rav Nissan Alpert offers a wonderful explanation. The only one way to sanctify Hashem's Name is by living the type of daily life that sanctifies His Name. If a person's eating is a *kiddush Hashem*, if his drinking is a *kiddush Hashem*, if his conduct in his business is a *kiddush Hashem*, then if he faces the ultimate test he will automatically make a *kiddush Hashem*, even at the cost of his life. It will practically happen by itself that Hashem's Name "will become sanctified." But if a person's life bears little or no connection to *kiddush Hashem*, it will not do much good to command him to "sanctify My Name." The concept will be too far removed.

When Rabbi Akiva was being tortured by the Romans, his skin flayed with iron combs, he started saying *Krias Shema*. His *talmidim* asked him how he could bear it, and he replied, "*Kol yamai*, all my days." His *whole life* was pointed here. This is what he meant. All his life had been one long act of *kiddush Hashem*. Every aspect of his life, the way he talked, the way he walked, the way he dressed, everything was *kiddush Hashem*. Therefore, the end only came naturally.

Rabbi Shmuel Bloom, in an article in the *Jewish Observer*, writes about Rabbi Moshe Sherer's testimony before Congress in 1961 in favor of government aid to private and parochial schools. The story made the front page of *The New York Times*.

When Rabbi Sherer returned from Washington, Rav Aharon Kotler told him, "More important than the funds that may be received by *yeshivos* was that you removed a *chillul Hashem*. Until now, Americans believed that only Catholics are in favor of religious education and that Jews are against religious education. Liberal Jews have always voiced their support for the public school system and their opposition to government aid to religious schools. Jews against religious education? That was a horrendous *chillul Hashem*. But you have changed that. Americans now know that committed Jews are in favor of religious education. That was a tremendous accomplishment."

Believe me, Rav Aharon Kotler was involved with many other *yeshivos* besides his own. He knew full well how all *yeshivos* were desperately starving for funds. But the life-giving flow of cash from Washington was secondary in his mind. First and foremost was the knowledge that a *chillul Hashem* had been removed, that a *kiddush Hashem* had been made. This is a powerful lesson to all of us. In everything we do, first and foremost we must make a *kiddush Hashem*.

Let His Name be sanctified.

TESHUVAH

Windows of Opportunity

EVERY ONCE IN A LONG WHILE, WE EXPERIENCE A YEAR unlike any other in memory, and we are convinced that the long-awaited time has finally come. *Mashiach* is on the doorstep at long last. But when it doesn't happen, we are disappointed and perplexed. We seek answers. How did we miss that opportunity? What could we have done differently?

The year 5751 (1991), for instance, was no ordinary year by any measure. A banner headline is the term applied to headlines that stretch across the entire width of a newspaper. In an average year, *The New York Times* runs five or six banner headlines. The record for banner headlines since the Second World War was 15 banner headlines in 1990. But in 1991, there were 40 banner headlines in the *Times*. It was not just another year.

The year began with a cloud hanging over our head. Iraq had invaded Kuwait, and we knew that ominous things loomed in the future of the Jewish people. The Allies set an ultimatum with a January 15 deadline. After that it would be war, a horrible and frightening prospect. But the alternative of allowing the tyrant's power to grow unchecked was perhaps even more frightening.

All over the world, Jewish people came together to pray for the safety of *Eretz Yisrael* as the deadline drew near. Parents with children in *Eretz Yisrael* suffered through a particular brand of anguish. Should they bring their children home? Should they allow them to stay? The torment and the anxiety were unforgettable.

And then came that fateful Thursday night, the night that the Iraqi Scud missiles began to fall on *Eretz Yisrael*. I remember driving down Park Heights Avenue in Baltimore when the reports were still unclear. Reporters were talking about the possibility of a biological warfare attack on Jerusalem, anthrax perhaps, expecting casualties in the hundreds if not more. I remember coming into the *beis midrash* and seeing the terror in people's eyes, the fright. What was going to be?

I also remember Purim of that year, the utter euphoria of a Purim on which the end of the war was announced. Of all days, the war ended on Purim. On the day of the Jewish calendar on which we were saved from national destruction thousands of years ago, we were saved again now. *Bayamim haheim bazman hazeh*, in those days and in our times. Thirty-nine Scuds had fallen on *Eretz Yisrael*, but only three people in the entire nation were killed. An angel was undoubtedly hovering over the encampment of the Jewish people, shielding them from harm. The miracles were open and undeniable.

That entire winter, while war raged in the Persian Gulf, the entrance to my *yeshivah* in Baltimore, Maryland was blocked and chained as a precaution against terrorist attacks. Now the obstructions were removed. In *Eretz Yisrael,* people ripped down the adhesive from their sealed rooms. The siege had been lifted. We were liberated.

That same year, 5751, we saw the fulfillment of the prophetic words that Hashem would "extract a nation from among a nation." We saw Ethiopian Jews snatched from the jaws of death. And we saw the Iron Curtain flung open and hundreds of thousands of Jews streaming out to freedom.

On Rosh Hashanah, we plead with Hashem "to remove the evil empire from the earth," and that was exactly what He did. For so many years I used to say those words while thinking of the Soviet Union, a corrupt and vindictive state predicated on denial of the Creator. Who ever believed it would collapse in our lifetimes? But in 5751, that is exactly what happened. It cracked, crumbled and collapsed. Then it was gone, *ke'ashan tichleh,* "vanished like a wisp of smoke."

It was truly a spectacular year, but it was also a year of profound disappointment. Many of us had believed that this would be the year *Mashiach* would come. All those signs, all those miracles — it just had to be the prelude to the final redemption. But it wasn't. *Mashiach* didn't come. In spite of everything, he never came.

What do you do with such a year? How do you view such a year? What did we do wrong? What did we do right? What can we learn for the future?

I think that in some ways the year 5751 may have been a microcosm of all Jewish history. Even more, it is a microcosm of the story of mankind, of each and every one of us. It is the story of Adam, the first human being.

The Midrash states that the story of Adam and Chavah parallels the history of the Jewish people, so let us take a closer look at the story of Adam and Chavah.

We all know the basic facts. The serpent tells Chavah to eat the forbidden fruit of the Tree of Knowledge for "on the day you eat it you will become like the Lord Who recognizes good and evil." The serpent is convincing, and he persuades

Chavah to eat the forbidden fruit. She then persuades Adam to eat it as well. And then "their eyes opened, and they realized they were naked."

The Midrash is puzzled by this last statement. Didn't they know they were naked all along? Even a blind person knows when he is naked. The answer, explains the Midrash, is that the Torah is not discussing physical nakedness. Rather, the Torah is stating that they felt spiritually denuded. Hashem had given them one *mitzvah*, just one solitary *mitzvah*, and they had transgressed it. And when they realized what had happened, they felt stripped of all worth, totally naked, totally devastated. One *mitzvah*, and they couldn't keep it.

But it goes much deeper than that. Stop and think for a moment. What was so unusual about that forbidden fruit? Was it infused with mystical powers? Was it supernatural in nature?

Not at all. Rabbi Pinchas ben Yair, quoted in the Midrash, assures us that it was an absolutely ordinary fruit, no different from any other fruit in the world. What set this fruit apart from other fruits was one thing and one thing only. Hashem had said, "Do not eat it." That was it, nothing more. But that should have been far more than enough.

The forbidden fruit was to be the conduit through which people learned that not everything in this world is accessible to them, that some things are off limits, that some things are beyond the scope of human comprehension. That was the singular characteristic of this fruit, that it was forbidden.

This was the issue the serpent directly attacked. You don't have to obey, he insisted. You're not robots. You have a mind of your own. You don't have to take instructions. You are human beings, and your scope is unlimited.

And so they ate the forbidden fruit, and they discovered that it was just an ordinary piece of fruit. Suddenly, an awful realization dawned on them. They realized that they had transgressed Hashem's command without expanding their horizons in any way. It had all been for naught. For this they had compromised their relationship with the Almighty? For a plain old fruit? And they felt naked, stripped down to a state of utter, utter worthlessness.

Rav Shimon Schwab was once called to a hospital to visit a man dying of tuberculosis. The man came from Vienna, where he had been raised in a religious family. But when he came to America, he abandoned his religion and lived without any restraints. When his son married a non-Jewish woman, however, he began to have second thoughts about what he had done. And now, on his deathbed, he wanted Rav Schwab to help him say *Viduy,* to help him confess his sins.

Halfway through *Viduy,* the man cried out, "Hashem! See my suffering. I was the greatest sinner. I wasted my life and the lives of my children. You gave me this great gift, and I squandered it away. And for what? What am I left with after all these years? Nothing at all. I was such a fool. Hashem! How can I appear before You?"

Rav Schwab sat by silently, with tears in his eyes, as the man poured out his bitter remorse. After a few minutes, the man was convulsed by a fit of violent coughing, and the nurses came running.

Seeing that the nurses needed to attend to their patient, Rav Schwab rose to his feet. "Take care of him," he said. "We can finish tomorrow."

Tomorrow never came for the man. He died in the middle of the night.

At the funeral, Rav Schwab was asked to give the eulogy. "I knew this man for only one day," he said. " I do not know what his life was like. But I do know one thing. He did *teshuvah.* I have never in my life seen a man do *teshuvah* with such sincerity."

The torment that man felt on his deathbed is reminiscent of the feeling Adam and Chavah experienced on that day. And that is the feeling that recurs again and again in the lives of countless millions of people every single day. We do things we shouldn't do, we say things we shouldn't say, and when it is over we take stock. Was it worth it? This is the special fruit? For this I had to transgress the commands of the Almighty? For this I had to sacrifice my honor? For this I had to break my ethical code? For this I had to give up my self-respect? And we feel naked, stripped of merit and dignity, utterly worthless.

So what is Hashem's response to this history-altering event? What does He say to Adam at this occasion?

Hashem responds with one word. "*Ayeka?*" He says. "Where are you, Adam?" He does not reproach the poor sinner. He does not castigate him. He wants to know where he is spiritually. He shows him that, in spite of the sin and the transgression, He still cares. He lets him know that there is still hope.

Our Sages tell us that *ayeka* also has an entirely different meaning. When read with alternate vowels it becomes *eichah*, which means, how could it be? *Eichah*, how could it be, is the plaintive cry, the pitiful groan that echoes through the *Book of Lamentations*. These two words, *ayeka* and *eichah*, are connected. Hashem says, *Ayeka?* Where are you? But He is also implying, *Eichah?* How could you? You have squandered your opportunities. You had so much, and you lost it.

This is where the Midrash finds the parallel between the story of Adam and the history of the Jewish people. We have had so many opportunities, so many gifts, and we squandered them. And still, Hashem tells us, "*Ayeka?*" Still, there is hope for us. Just as Hashem installed Adam in the Garden of Eden and gave him one *mitzvah,* He also installed our people in *Eretz Yisrael,* that Garden of Eden on earth, and gave us *mitzvos.* Just as Adam transgressed and was expelled from Eden with the word *ayeka,* so too were the Jewish people expelled from the land with the word *eichah.*

Both words apply in both cases. Adam's *ayeka* contains an implicit *eichah* and our *eichah* contains an implicit *ayeka. Ayeka?* Where are you? I am still concerned about you. But *eichah?* How could you do this? What a shame it is.

I believe that at the end of 5751 Hashem looked back at the year and said, "*Eichah?* How could it be? Such a phenomenal year. Such a year of opportunity. How could you let it pass without seizing the moment?"

I believe that this year, like certain other years in Jewish history, was a window of opportunity. This was a year when secular Israelis on the streets of Tel Aviv said, "*Ra'inu et yad Hashem.* We saw Hashem's hand." This could have been the year of *Mashiach.* But nothing happens, and Hashem said, "*Eichah?* How could it be?"

Reb Mendel of Rimanov was once walking with a group of *chassidim* and they saw a child sitting behind a tree and crying.

"Why are you crying, my child?" asked Reb Mendele.

"We're playing hide-and-go-seek," said the child, "and it is my turn to hide. So I'm hiding. But no one is looking for me. No one is interested in finding me." And he burst into tears again.

Reb Mendele turned to his *chassidim* and said, "Do you hear what this child said? That is how Hashem feels. No one is looking for Him. No one is seeking Him. He is there, but no one is coming."

But *eichah* is also *ayeka.* No matter how far we have strayed, no matter how many opportunities we have missed, Hashem always holds out His hand to us. There is always hope.

So let us get back to 5751. In what way did we miss our chance? Or to put it more bluntly, how did we blow it?

Sad to say, as much as things changed, things remain the same. I think that precisely the same sin that got us into this mess called *galus* in the first place is still keeping us here. Our Sages kept no secrets from us. They told us exactly what this *galus* is all about. It is about *sinas chinam*, unwarranted hatred. It is about people hating each other for absolutely no reason, a gratuitous sin. Apparently, this is also one of the major themes of Yom Kippur.

Why are we forbidden to wear leather shoes on Yom Kippur? Our Sages tell us that the Torah wants us to emulate the *malachei hashares*, the ministering angels, who are without jealousy or competitiveness. Since angels need no shoes, we connect with them symbolically when we take off our shoes. Hopefully, this connection will lead us to emulate their spiritual qualities as well. Be like the angels, says the Torah. Forget the petty jealousies and the competitiveness that can take over our lives if we allow it to happen.

Moreover, our Sages explain, removing our shoes reminds us that Yosef was sold into slavery by his brothers for a pair of shoes. Yom Kippur has a dual theme. It is a day of transcendent majesty, with the *Kohen Gadol* performing the hallowed *Avodah* and even entering the Holy of Holies. Oh, what a sight it was! "*Ashrei ayin ra'asa kol eileh*," we say. "Fortunate is the eye that saw all of this."

What happened? Where has all this majesty gone?

Avonos avoseinu hecherivu naveh, the sins of our fathers destroyed it. *Eileh ezkerah*, we say, these I recall and weep. And we go on to describe the torture and execution of the Ten Martyrs in the aftermath of the destruction of the *Beis Hamikdash*. Why did all this happen? Because of a national weakness that has plagued the Jewish people since the time Yosef was sold into slavery by his brothers for a pair of shoes. Because of jealousy and competitiveness among brothers. That's what brought it on. And so we take off our shoes.

Jealousy and competitiveness among brothers, neighbors and friends, among people of one flesh and blood who should be living together in peace and harmony, that is what has brought us to this sorry state. *Sinas chinam*, unwarranted hatred, is such a pervasive part of our lives.

Think about it. How often do we argue with our spouses about matters that are really trivial? The issue is winning. How many times does it happen in *shul* or in our other relationships? Winning. That's what it's about. Winning isn't everything, they say in America, it's the only thing. Unfortunately, we've swallowed this philosophy hook, line and sinker. Win at home. Win in the workplace. Win in *shul*. Win in the community.

This has got to stop. We have to stop trying to win. People can agree to disagree without falling out with each other. They can disagree vehemently, but they don't have to hate each other because of it. There is no need for snide remarks or condescension.

Listen to this letter that was sent to the editor of the *Jewish Observer*. "We are a group of students from the Ari Crown Jewish Academy of Chicago. Our class has a mixed population, ranging from Orthodox to non-religious. Many of the students in our class have a public school background and they sacrificed much to come to a Jewish high school. In spite of our trying our hardest to keep *mitzvot*, we are at times made to feel like outcasts by the Orthodox community. The boys in our class wear knit *kipot*, and the girls may wear pants when not in school. But we are still Jews, Jews who are trying to grow and become better Jews. Many of us used to be concerned about how gentiles would react to our wearing *kipot*. We used to feel self-conscious about being seen in *kipot* in public. Now we feel more scorned by our fellow Jews when we enter kosher restaurants or neighborhood stores because our *kipot* are knit and not black velvet."

This is what it's about. The problem exists on all sides, the right wing, the left wing, the center wing. It is, unfortunately, universal. Intolerance, pettiness, sanctimonious competition, gratuitous hatred. It has got to stop. We've got to stop bashing each other. No matter what we wear on our heads, whether *kipot* or black hats, we're all brothers and sisters.

Rav Chaim Shmulevitz was a *talmid* of the Novardoker Yeshivah when he married the daughter of Rav Leizer Yudel Finkel, the *Rosh Yeshivah* of the Mirrer Yeshivah; eventually, he succeeded his father-in-law and served for many years as *rosh yeshivah* in his own right. The wedding was a meeting between these two grand *yeshivos,* and it was a gala affair.

During the wedding, some of the Mirrer *talmidim* wanted to sing *grammen*, light, humorous verse often sung at weddings. The Novardoker *talmidim*, however, felt this was too frivolous and undignified. The Mirrer Yeshivah was far from a party house, but the Novardokers set an even stricter standard. Light verse at a wedding? Scandalous. One thing led to another, and soon, the atmosphere was poisoned by tension and friction.

Rav Yerucham Levovitz, the Mashgiach of the Mirrer Yeshivah, got up on a chair. "What is this?" he cried out. "We're all brothers. Let's embrace and dance together."

What is this business? Novardok and Mir fighting? It cannot be allowed. We are all brothers. We have to embrace and dance together. We have to stop this *sinas chinam*, this unwarranted hatred, if we want *Mashiach* to come anytime soon. *Sinas chinam* can slam the brakes on redemption even in a year as spectacular as 5751.

But I think we also squandered that special year by missing the opportunity to do *teshuvah*. Rav Yitzchak Hutner defines teshuvah as "not only improving but actually changing." It is not enough merely to become better. We have to become different. We have to undergo fundamental changes.

One would have thought that after a year like 5751, we would have changed, at least slightly. And we did not change at all. The Jewish people had a near-death experience. A large segment of our people was on the verge of annihilation. We were in greater danger than at any time since the Holocaust. People are supposed to change in circumstances such as these — but we didn't.

I recently heard a story about a great tragedy that happened in a certain community. A vibrant 35 year-old woman, a mother of young children, suddenly died of an aneurysm. It rocked the community. One day during the *shivah*, people were sitting in the house, and the grieving husband had to step out for a few minutes. While they waited for him to return, people spoke to each other in hushed tones about the enormity of what had befallen this family.

"After this," one woman said, "my husband and I have reached a decision. That trip to Europe we've been putting off again and again? Well, we're not putting it off any more. This summer, we're off to Europe."

That's a Jewish reaction? Is that what we're meant to learn from such a tragedy in our midst? Eat, drink and be merry, for tomorrow we may die?

Listen instead to a completely different outlook. In the same community, a woman is in the hospital with terminal cancer. They have stopped all chemotherapy, in effect conceding defeat. The woman's rabbi comes to visit her in the hospital.

"Rabbi, I want to tell you something," she says, "The year and a half since I've had cancer has changed my life. I look at my husband differently. I treat my children differently. I am a different person."

The rabbi looks at her and decides to pose a very audacious question. "If this year was so meaningful to you, let me ask you this. If you had your choice between having the cancer and the difference it made in your life, or not having the cancer, what would you choose?"

The woman looks him right in the eye and says, "Rabbi, the cancer has taught me what life is all about. This last year and a half was the only time in my life I have truly lived. If it's a choice between having the cancer and my earlier oblivious life, I would choose the cancer."

This woman grew from her encounter with death, but did we grow from ours? We faced national death in 5751, but we're virtually unchanged.

A rabbi told me he was in a Jewish cemetery and saw an entire section of tombstones on which bowling balls were engraved. The tombstones were inscribed, "We lived to bowl." Bowling balls! We lived to bowl! Incredible. We snicker at such stupidity. But truth be told, what will they put on our tombstones? What did we live for? Will they engrave logos of our businesses on our tombstones? Pictures of our houses? Would that be more appropriate?

So how do we seize the moment? How do we capitalize on those auspicious moments when we can set our own destiny? How can we squeeze through those windows of opportunity?

Let us go back again to that fateful year 5751. On January 14, the day before the war broke out, the renowned Dayan Dunner of England, asked Rav Eliezer Shach, "What should we tell the people in America, Europe and England? They want to do *teshuvah*. They want to do something. What should we tell them?"

"Tell them," said Rav Shach, "to make small but meaningful pledges for limited periods, from now until Pesach. For instance, they should not pledge not to speak *lashon hara* ever again for the rest of their lives. Let them undertake not to speak *lashon hara* from now until Pesach. One step at a time. Let it be small, well defined and limited. But do something." Rav Shach paused for a moment. "I'll tell you a secret. Do you know what I took upon myself this past Yom Kippur? I took upon myself to say *Bircas Hamazon* from a *siddur* until Pesach. But only when I'm at home."

Do you hear what Rav Shach, the *Rosh Yeshivah* of Ponevezh, one of the *gedolei hador*, took upon himself on Yom Kippur? *Bircas Hamazon* from a *siddur*. But only at home, and only until Pesach. Do something small, something limited, but seize the moment. Grasp the opportunity.

On Yom Kippur, we say, "*Avinu Malkeinu*, Our Father, our King, do not send us away empty-handed." I once heard an interesting interpretation of these words from Rav Chaim Dov Keller. What we are in effect saying is, Help me, Hashem, that I should not walk away with nothing this Yom Kippur. Let some of its inspiration remain with me afterwards. Don't let me fall into the trap of business as usual two days after Yom Kippur. Let me seize the moment.

Looking back at the year 5751, I think we can take some encouragement from a number of things. For one, that year proved to anyone who had any question as to the efficacy of prayer, that prayer works; that Hashem listens when we pray. While we may have to be reminded that He listens, because we don't always get the answers we want, who can doubt that He listened to our prayers in 5751 and saved us? Hashem always listens. He's always interested.

Rav Shimon Schwab relates a rather bizarre incident. Many years ago, he was standing at a bus stop in Baltimore in front of a Catholic church. A Jewish woman came out of the church, and seeing a rabbi, she walked over to him.

"Rabbi," she said, "you're probably wondering what a Jewish woman is doing in a Catholic church. Well, let me tell you, those Catholics, they have something that Judaism doesn't have, something that's just wonderful."

"Really?" said Rabbi Schwab. "And what's that?"

"It's the confessional," she said. "You sit in this booth, and the priest is sitting on the other side of the partition. You say, 'Forgive me, Father, for I have sinned.' The priest says, 'You are forgiven.' And presto. Forgiveness. You're forgiven, and you feel wonderful. Judaism doesn't have that."

"Madam, you are quite mistaken," he said. "Judaism certainly does have confession. Three times a day, we say, 'Selach lanu ... Forgive us, our Father, for we have sinned.' We have Viduy on Yom Kippur. What do you mean, Judaism doesn't have confession?"

"Rabbi, you don't understand," she replied. "At the Catholic church, someone is listening."

"Madam, you don't understand," said Rav Schwab. "The Jewish people also have Someone Who is listening. Always. And not a mere flesh-and-blood human who doesn't have the power of forgiveness, but the Creator of the Universe Himself."

This is what we must remember, that Hashem is always listening.

The most important lesson out of the unbelievable year 5751, however, is the amazing power of a people united. I truly believe that what saved the day was our coming together as a community with one focused purpose in mind. I truly believe that Hashem responded to the voice of the united community.

The *Meshech Chochmah* writes that although the Jews in Egypt worshipped idols and didn't keep the *mitzvah* of *milah*, they loved each other and did not speak *lashon hara*. Therefore, since they were united, Hashem performed miracles for them.

In 5751 as well, Hashem performed miracles for us because we were united; because Jews the world over were polite and courteous to each other; because they forgot their petty squabbles; because they came together to pray and learn as a community. That's what carried the day.

A former *talmid* of the Mirrer Yeshivah told me that when Jewish families and *yeshivos* were scattering in all directions during the German invasion of Poland, the Mirrer Yeshivah made a deliberate decision to stay together as a group. On Simchas Torah, they traveled *en masse* to Vilna. From Vilna, they traveled together through Russia, across Siberia and all the way to Shanghai, China.

Rav Chaim Shmulevitz writes that in Shanghai some of the *talmidim* wanted to organize a smaller group which would learn separately in a room off the *beis midrash*. Rav Chaim was against it. "If you do this thing," he told them, "you won't be protected by the merit of the entire *yeshivah* as a group. The only thing that is going to save this *yeshivah* is being a *tzibbur*, a single unit, a community.

That's the lesson of 5751. Forget the jealousy. Forget the competitiveness. Forget the dissension. Come together as a single united community.

A proctor once supervised a final exam administered to a

large class in law school.

"You have exactly two hours to complete this exam," the proctor told the class. "These are the instructions of your professor. At the end of the allotted time, the exam is over. If your paper is not handed in exactly two hours from the beginning of the exam, you fail."

Properly warned, the students all handed in their papers within the two-hour limit, with the exception of one student. He took an additional 10 minutes to work on the exam. When he was finished, he walked up to the proctor and said, "Here's my paper."

"I told you," said the proctor, "that if you hand in your paper even one minute late, you fail. Didn't you hear me?"

The student looked at the proctor. "Tell me, do you know who I am?"

"I don't know who you are," said the proctor, "and I don't particularly care. You're late, and you've failed."

"Do you know my name?" asked the student

"No, I don't know your name, and I don't want to know your name."

"Good," said the student, and he shoved his paper in among the completed exams piled high on the desk. "Have a nice day."

This amusing story is, of course, not exactly analogous to the subject at hand. Hashem most certainly does know who we are and our names. But the message of the story is unbelievably powerful. If we subsume ourselves into a larger group, we can get away with a lot. If you're part of the community, if you work for the community, if you are devoted to the community, if you promote solidarity and love and kindness and tolerance in the community, then you are protected by the community.

The *Zohar* tells us that when the Shunamite woman built a small private room for Elisha, he asked her in gratitude, "Can I do something for you? Do you need me to speak for you to the authorities? Do you need me to speak for you to the king?"

The *Zohar* explains that this exchange took place on Rosh Hashanah. Elisha was asking the woman if he could intercede on her behalf with the Almighty.

And what did the woman answer? *"Besoch ami anochi yosheves.* I dwell among my people." I don't need special intervention, because I am among my people. I enjoy the protection of the community.

Rav Yisrael Salanter gives us the final key to gaining acquittal on Yom Kippur. Every single person as an individual, Rav Yisrael explains, can achieve the merit of the community on his own. How can he do that? By working for the community. If a person is community minded, if the community comes to rely on him, then he as an individual has all the merits of a community, and Hashem will actually perform miracles for him.

This is the key to success on Yom Kippur. Become a community person. You don't have to become a high-profile public person if you don't feel comfortable with it. Every institution, every community organization is starving for help. There is something each and every one of use can contribute, whether it be financial, whether it be material, whether it be volunteer work, whether it be behind the scenes work. We can all become community people in our own different ways.

Give to the community. Promote the community. Become a community person, and as Rav Yisrael assures us, you will personally enjoy the benefits and the protection that are reserved for the community. There is nothing that Hashem would not do for the community. And there is nothing He would not do for you.

Suffering and Forgiveness

THERE WAS ONCE A MAN WHO, DURING HIS PREPARA-
tions for Yom Kippur, decided that he needed very
much to do or see something that would inspire him
to do *teshuvah*. He thought and thought and finally settled on
the idea that seeing the great Rebbe Reb Elimelech of
Lizhensk, the author of *Noam Elimelech*, perform the *kaparos*
ritual would be a transcendent experience. In his mind, he
conjured up an image of the holy sage, tears streaming from
his eyes as he brandished a white rooster over his head. It
stirred him to his very soul.

The man gathered up his courage and asked the *rebbe* for
permission to be present for the *kaparos*.

"You're looking to be inspired, aren't you?" said the *rebbe*.
"Then don't watch my *kaparos*. Go to the Jewish innkeeper in
such-and-such a village. Watch what he does for *kaparos*."

Somewhat reluctantly, the man took the *rebbe's* advice and set off for that village. Along the way, he was consumed by curiosity. Who could this Jew be? Could he be one of the *lamed vav tzaddikim*, the 36 hidden righteous people who are the pillars of the world?

When he arrived in the village and met the Jewish innkeeper, he was sorely disappointed. The innkeeper was a vulgar fellow. He didn't seem to be a scholar, nor did he appear to be particularly pious. At best, he was just an ordinary Jew. What in the world could the *rebbe* have wanted him to learn from this Jew?

"I've come to watch you do *kaparos*," the man told the innkeeper. "Do you mind?"

The innkeeper gave him a strange look and shrugged his shoulders indifferently.

The night before Yom Kippur, the innkeeper told his wife, "Bring me my ledgers." A minute later, he was holding two worn account books in his callused hands. As the visitor watched in amazement, the innkeeper opened them and began to take stock of his life.

One ledger contained a meticulous accounting of all his failures and shortcomings during the year gone by. Every time he failed to say *Krias Shema* in its proper time, every time he missed Minchah, every time he spoke *lashon hara*, every *aveirah* he had committed throughout the year, large and small, all of it was recorded in the book.

The second ledger recorded all the suffering he had endured throughout the year. All his business setbacks, all his disappointments, all the indignities that he had suffered at the hands of other people, all the insults and hurtful remarks he had endured, all the grief and sorrow he had witnessed in the community, the widows and orphans, the sick children, the unemployed, the starving, all of these were recorded in the second ledger.

"*Ribono Shel Olam,*" he cried out after he had finished reviewing the accounts. "We made a deal last year. I promised to improve, and You were supposed to give me a good year. But look at these ledgers. Neither of us has kept to the deal. So I'll make You another deal right now. I will forgive You for what You've done, and You forgive me for what I've done."

The next morning, when it came time to say *kaparos*, the innkeeper took the two ledgers and brandished them over his head as he said, "*Zeh chalifasi ...* This is my replacement ..."

I'm reluctant to repeat this story, because it almost borders on the blasphemous. The *Ribono Shel Olam* certainly doesn't need our forgiveness. I believe, though, that it conveys important lessons, that it delves into the human mind and addresses some very real issues.

First, we immediately see the absolute conviction of this simple Jew that Hashem controls and guides the world, from the greatest things to the most minute. This, after all, is the underlying theme of this time of the year. Where does it all lead to? After the 30 days of Elul, after Rosh Hashanah, after the *Aseres Yemei Teshuvah*, after the whole day of Yom Kippur has passed, after we reach the very end of Ne'ilah, what is the climax? What words do we shout out when we stand at the very pinnacle of repentance? "*Hashem Hu Ha'Elokim. Hashem Hu Ha'Elokim.*" That's what it all comes down to. *Hashem Hu Ha'Elokim.* Hashem is the Lord. This is His world, all of it and everything and everyone it contains.

Rav Chaim Volozhiner offers an interesting insight into the words *Hashem Hu Ha'Elokim. Hashem* is the Name which connotes His mastery over the vast cosmic issues of the world: famine, war, peace. floods. It relates to His macromanagement, if you will. *Elokim,* on the other hand, connotes His mastery over the little things in life that people sometimes tend to attribute to happenstance. It relates to His micromanagement of the world, to *hashgachah pratis* in the fullest meaning of the word. This is what *Hashem Hu Ha'Elokim* conveys to us, that both are one and the same. Everything comes from one Source.

But there is a much deeper lesson in this curious little Chassidic story. We see that there is a preliminary step that must be taken before we can do *teshuvah*. Before a person can do *teshuvah* he must first make peace with the *Ribono Shel Olam*. He must first settle his grievances and come to terms with Hashem, because an alienated person cannot do *teshuvah*. A person who is angry at Hashem cannot do *teshuvah*.

A woman once sought my advice about prayer. She told me that she had always found prayer a wonderful and exhilarating experience. She felt she was communicating with Hashem. She felt close to Him. But now she's lost it. She no longer feels the closeness. Instead, she feels that she's just doing it by rote. What should she do?

How admirable, I thought, that a person should be so worried about things like maintaining a high level of prayer. And so I began to discuss the problem with this woman, and I discovered that modes of prayer were not her problem. She was angry at Hashem. Her husband had suffered a long period of illness. Her father had passed away years before without ever having seen his grandchildren. She had so wanted her father to hold her children on his lap, but it didn't happen. The death of her father had left an aching void inside her, and she was angry at Hashem. She was disappointed with life. So how could she pray if she was angry? How could she pray if she had grievances? How could she open up to Him? How could she do *teshuvah*?

So how do we deal with the disappointments and tragedies of life? How do we deal with these feelings of alienation, of distance from Hashem? How do we make up with Him, so to speak?

There are actually two major roots of alienation. The first derives from the big things in life, the overwhelming tragedies, the calamities that sometimes befall us and other people, the slings and arrows of outrageous fortune. The second derives from the smaller things, the day-to-day disappointments, the insults, the insensitive remarks of our colleagues, the aggravations we sometimes endure from our spouses and children, the inescapable assault of daily life.

Let us first address the calamities of life. Even if we ourselves have been fortunate, we are surrounded by calamity in our community.

A pharmacist from a religious neighborhood in Brooklyn recently called me. "What should I do?" he asked me. "I see too much sickness. I'm dispensing drugs for the worst type of diseases, and I'm not talking about strep throats and ear infections. It's just too much. I had to fill a prescription for a father who told me he was teaching his 5-year-old son to say *Kaddish*. I went to *shul* this morning, and cried all through *Shacharis*." He paused, and I heard him crying. "So what should I do? Maybe I should get out of this business. It upsets me too much. I don't know what to do."

How indeed can we deal with such calamity all around us? What does the Almighty want from us? There are no simple answers. But it ultimately comes down to faith. In the end, all we have are *emunah* and *bitachon*. We must trust that Hashem has our best interests in mind. And we must realize that human beings are incapable of understanding the ways of Hashem, that we cannot begin to fathom His master plan.

This is one of the vital messages our Sages wanted us to extract from Yom Kippur. They wanted us to get beyond these feelings of alienation. They wanted us to deal with it, to come to terms with it.

In the crucial waning hours of Yom Kippur, during Minchah, we read the story of Yonah. What is the message of this story? How does it relate to Yom Kippur?

You know, *Sefer Yonah* really ends after the first three *perakim*. We all know the story of Yonah. Hashem sends him on a mission of prophecy to the Assyrian city of Nineveh to tell its people to do *teshuvah*. But Yonah doesn't want to go, and so, he flees. It doesn't do him any good, though. Ultimately, he does deliver the prophecy to Nineveh, and its people do *teshuvah*. Thus concludes the third chapter, and essentially, the story of Yonah comes to an end. And then there is the fourth and final chapter, which appears almost as an afterthought, almost as an epilogue.

The fourth chapter begins with Yonah declaring, "I'm very angry." He was angry with what Hashem had caused him to do. He was upset that the Assyrians had been inspired to do *teshuvah*, while his own Jewish people had not. What an indictment of the Jewish people! Yonah realized that he had brought it on. He had no desire to go on living, and he asked Hashem to take his life. "I would prefer death to life," he cries out in anguish.

This is a noble act in the tradition of earlier Jewish prophets who preferred to die rather than witness the downfall of the Jewish people. Moshe Rabbeinu had reacted in the same way. "Remove me from Your book," he had said. And now his words are echoed by Yonah.

And Hashem replies, "Are you really angry?" A rhetorical question. And the scene fades out. We are not told about Yonah's response. The scene shifts. Yonah leaves Nineveh and encamps outside the city, hoping against hope that the *teshuvah* movement in Nineveh will sputter and run out of gas. Perhaps the Assyrians would return to their wicked ways, and the indictment against the Jewish people would be torn up.

As he sits and waits, Yonah suffers terribly from the broiling sun. He is wracked by pain and beset by distress. Miraculously, a tree sprouts from the ground nearby and provides him with delicious shade. He is ecstatic. Then Hashem sends in an extraordinarily hot wind which destroys the shade tree. Yonah is once again at the mercy of the merciless sun. He cries out in anguish, "I would prefer death to life."

Those are familiar words. The very same words he spoke when he did not want to witness the downfall of the Jewish people he now speaks when he suffers the loss of the shade tree.

And what does Hashem reply? "Are you really angry?" The same response He had made to the earlier request.

The irony is inescapable. Yonah is upset about two things. He's upset about a grand theological issue. He is upset that the Assyrians are on the verge of earning Divine forgiveness while the Jewish people still wallow in their sinfulness. He is angry, very angry. He wants to die. And he is also upset that he is suffering physically, that his shade tree has shriveled and died. Again, he is angry. And he wants to die. And both times, Hashem tells him, "Are you really angry?"

What is going on? What is Hashem trying to tell Yonah?

It appears that Hashem is demonstrating to Yonah that it's impossible for him to understand the Divine plan. Hashem is demonstrating to Yonah that he is no more than a mere human being. Put things into perspective, Hashem is saying. So you have grand theological problems? You don't understand *hashgachah*? You don't understand Hashem's relationship with pagans and Jews? Do you know what your problem is, Yonah? You are a human being, a physical creature. You get upset over physical discomfort, and you find delight in shade. What is more fleeting in life than shade? So if you are just a plain and simple human being, how do you expect to understand the ways of Hashem?

That's what's happening with Yonah. He has theological problems. He doesn't understand life. And Hashem lets him know that questions are fine, as long as they do not interfere with faith, as long as they do not distance a person from Hashem.

Rabbi Moshe Eisemann, in his insightful work on *Sefer Iyov,* points out that we find two different reactions to tragedy in the Torah. Aharon lost two of his sons, and how did he react? *Vayidom Aharon.* And Aharon was totally silent. He accepted it with no questions asked. Iyov also lost his children, and how did he react? With questions. Questions and questions and more questions. But Hashem was not displeased with Iyov. It was all right for him to have questions, because he never lost his fundamental faith. He wanted to be

close. He wanted to understand, and he was finding it difficult. But he never lost faith in the existence of Hashem.

The Satmar Rav asks an interesting question. The Torah
tells us (*Vayikra* 16:30), "For on this very day He will
absolve you to purify you; you shall become pure in front of
Hashem." What does the second part of this verse add to the
first part? It seems redundant.

These last words, explains the Satmar Rav, refer to such
sins that are "in front of Hashem." No one else knows about
them, because they are between a person and Hashem. Sins,
such as questions deep down about the existence of
Hashem, are what we have to deal with on Yom Kippur. We
have to come to grips with these questions. We cannot come
into Yom Kippur insecure in our personal relationship with
Hashem. We cannot come into Yom Kippur without removing
this fundamental sin from ourselves.

Strong words. Do you know when and to whom they were
said? They were said right after the war to Jews who had just
recently been liberated from the concentration camps. And
in front of these people, the courageous Satmar Rav got up
and declared, "You may not have any doubts. You may not
harbor questions in your heart. You have gone through the
worst. You have gone through *Gehinnom*. You have seen
men, women and children go up in flames. You have lived
through a nightmare, but in spite of everything, you must
know that it is forbidden to doubt Hashem."

Now why would the Satmar Rav choose this particular
topic to speak about to this particular audience? Couldn't he
have chosen something less painful, less provocative? Why
rub salt on their wounds? Perhaps he should have waited
until the people were ready to hear something like that.

The answer is no. The Satmar Rav knew there was no time
to waste. If these people wanted to do *teshuvah*, they had to
deal with it right away. Naturally, those people had the advantage of hearing these words from the Satmar Rav, who was
the paragon of *emunah*. But all people in all circumstances

must deal with it before they can possibly do *teshuvah*.

The Klausenberger Rebbe , speaking before Kol Nidrei in the displaced persons camps, took out a *machzor* and began to go through the list of *ashamnus* and *al cheits*.

Ashamnu? he began. Doesn't apply to us. We're guilty? Of what? We're not guilty. Not after what we went through. *Bagadnu*. We rebelled. We weren't loyal. Doesn't apply to us. We were loyal. *Gazalnu*. We stole. Stole? Doesn't apply to us. Stole from whom? Stole what? What was there to steal? *Dibarnu dofi*. We spoke. Doesn't apply to us. Who had strength to speak? The rest of the *ashamnus?* Doesn't apply to us.

Now the *al cheits*. *Be'ones uveratzon*. We did anything willingly? *Begilui arayos*. Who had strength? All the *al cheits*. Doesn't apply to us. Every single one of them doesn't apply.

The Klausenberger Rebbe, who lost his wife and 11 children, closed the *machzor* and said, "There's one *aveirah* they didn't write on these lists. Where is the *al cheit* of losing our *emunah*? Because we did lose our *emunah*. When we went to sleep at night, how many of us hoped and prayed we wouldn't wake up the next morning? We lost our *emunah*. And when we woke up the next morning and had to carry those who didn't make it through the night, how many looked at them wishing it had been them? We lost our *emunah*."

The Klausenberger Rebbe, that paragon of *emunah* and *bitachon*, was trying to convey to his people that if they could not recover their *emunah*, they could never do *teshuvah*. And that's the lesson of Yonah, that human beings cannot understand everything, that sometimes we just have to accept. We just have to have this *emunah* and *bitachon* that Hashem has our best interests in mind.

Furthermore, the story of Yonah also teaches us that we must serve Hashem on His terms, not ours, that He sets the agenda, not we. Yonah was convinced he knew the right way to serve Hashem. He didn't feel his mission to Nineveh was the right thing to do. It would cause trouble, create a *chilul*

Hashem, an indictment against the Jewish people. Yonah didn't like the plan.

But that was wrong. It is not up to Yonah to decide how best to serve Hashem. It is up to Hashem.

Think about it for a moment. Don't we do this all the time? Oh, I would be a much better person and a much better Jew, we tell ourselves, if only Hashem would do things my way. If only he would let me rewrite the script a little bit. If only I had the right job, I would learn so much more. If only I were in a different profession, then I'd be able to serve Hashem better. If only I had money, then I would be a different person. If only I had more children. If only I were married. If only this. If only that. If only.

At some point in our lives, however, we should come to the realization that ours is the role that Hashem has chosen for us. Of course, we're not supposed to throw up our hands in futility and be fatalistic about it. Hashem wants us to make *hishtadlus*, to try and improve our lot. But there are limits. There has to come a point where a person says to himself, "This is it. This is who I am, and this is where I am. This is my wife, these are my children, this is my job, this is my city, these are my neighbors and this is what I have to do."

A person cannot presume to dictate to Hashem. That is not the role of a true servant of Hashem. When we declare Hashem our King, it must be more than lip service. The king sets the agenda, not the servant. We don't set the agenda.

Rav Yisrael Salanter makes this point in a famous parable.

A king had assigned a new ambassador to a neighboring country. "Before you go," said the king to the ambassador, "I want to give you one instruction. Whatever you do, make no bets, no wagers. That's all I want from you. Make absolutely no wagers with anyone at all."

The ambassador arrives in the other kingdom and goes to the palace to pay his respects to the king. The king takes one look at him and gets red in the face.

"I am outraged," he shouted. "Why did your king send me

a hunchback for an ambassador?"

The ambassador was shocked. "A hunchback? Me, a hunchback? I'm not a hunchback."

"Oh, yes you are," says the king. "Anyone can see you're a hunchback."

"Pardon me, your majesty," said the ambassador. "Far be it from me to disagree with a king, but I know what I am and what I am not. And I most definitely am not a hunchback."

"Very well then," said the king. "We will prove it one way or the other. I will bet you a million rubles. A million rubles says that you are a hunchback. Take off your shirt right here in front of the court and let the people decide for themselves whether or not you are a hunchback. If they say you are not, the million rubles is yours."

The ambassador was at a loss. The words of his king rang clearly in his memory. Make no wagers, he had said. But this was surely different. There was no risk here. After all, he was certainly not a hunchback. But still, the king had said no wagers. What was he to do? And then he had an idea. He would make the wager but give the money to the king. Then the king would surely be pleased.

With this resolve in mind, the ambassador ripped off his shirt and paraded himself in front of the court. The courtiers all whispered to each other and nodded their heads. He was right. This man was not a hunchback.

The king accepted defeat and gave the ambassador his million rubles.

The ambassador returned to his own kingdom and brought his million rubles to the king.

"Here, your majesty," he said. "I won this for you."

"Do you mean to say that you made a wager?" asked the king. "Didn't I expressly forbid it?"

"Yes, your majesty," said the ambassador. "But there was no risk, and I won a million rubles for you."

"You fool," said the king. "Why didn't you obey me? I had made a 5 million-ruble bet with my neighbor the king that he couldn't get you to take off your shirt in public. You may have won a million rubles for me, but you made me lose five million."

In our lives, too, no matter how compelling our reasoning may seem to us, no matter how sure we are that we know what to do, we have to follow the rules. We can't set the agenda. We have to learn acceptance.

Moreover, we have to learn to accept not only the major conditions that Hashem has ordained for us but also the day-to-day aggravations and annoyances, the slights we must endure from other people. Those are also part of Hashem's plan. And if we learn to accept that, we would improve our relationship not only with Hashem but also with our fellow man.

For example, let us take the issue of revenge. If someone insults or injures us, the Torah forbids us to take revenge. Obviously, this means we shouldn't even want to take revenge. If the Torah doesn't want us to, then we ourselves shouldn't want to either. How is this possible? How can we overcome the internal, unexpressed desire to take revenge?

Listen to what the Chinuch says, "Don't plot and scheme to avenge yourself on him, because he is not the problem. He's just a tool of Heaven. What's happening to you is because Hashem wants it to happen to you. You have caused it; he did not."

The Chinuch then brings the classic example of King David and Shimi ben Geira. When Absalom usurped the throne and King David was forced to flee, Shimi ben Geira decided to take advantage of the deposed king's vulnerability, and he cursed him roundly. King David's attendants were enraged, but the king restrained them. "Let him curse," said the king. "Hashem is telling him to do it." It is not Shimi. It is Hashem.

When such things happen to us, we must also remember this lesson. The cause of our misery is not really the person who is doing it. What power does he have over me? No, it's Hashem Who is doing it. And it is because it is coming to me.

I know that this is not an easy thing to do. It's definitely easier said than done. I actually know this from bitter experience. Last Rosh Hashanah, I decided to work on these very issues. I resolved to ingrain within myself a profound belief that *Hashem Hu Ha'Elokim,* that He controls every aspect of my life, that anything that happens to me, large or small, emanates directly from Him. Nothing anyone could say or do to me would offend me, because I would immediately recognize it as a message from Heaven.

It didn't take long for Hashem to test me. It just so happened that the regular *baal tefillah* was not available for Minchah, and I was asked to take his place. Now, I am not exactly famous for my skills as a *baal tefillah,* but like most of us, I was always convinced I could do a good job if given the opportunity. So here I am standing before the *amud* on Yom Kippur, and let me tell you, it is not nearly as easy as it seems. I managed to get through the hour and a half of Minchah, and then I returned to my seat much relieved. Two more hours for Ne'ilah, then came Maariv, and Yom Kippur was over.

Right after Maariv, a fellow comes over to me and says, "You know, you embarrassed yourself with that Minchah. Have a good year."

I was upset. I was angry at the fellow for offending me. I was disconcerted about this inauspicious start of my new year. Was this what the coming year would be like?

The person called me later and asked me to forgive him, and I did. I forgave him, but I was still bothered. Actually, I was bothered that it bothered me when I should have felt acceptance. I should have understood that "Hashem told him to do it," and I should have accepted it as a *kaparah,* as something that was in my best interest.

I should have taken comfort from the words of Ibn Ezra in *Bereishis.* When Yosef is born, Rachel says, "*Assaf Hashem es cherpasi.* Hashem gathered in my humiliation." What does this expression mean?

Ibn Ezra explains that Hashem saw Rachel humiliated by other women during all those years when the *midas hadin* did not allow her to have a child of her own. She suffered when women wheeled their baby carriages past her. She suffered when women made insensitive remarks in her presence. She suffered when women showed off their babies in front of her. Finally, Hashem "gathered in" all Rachel's humiliating experiences and placed them on the scale against the *midas hadin*. All her humiliation tipped the scale in her favor, and she could finally have a baby of her own.

We can all take comfort in this idea. All those humiliations, all those little pinpricks of life, all those disappointments, they all count for something. They help us balance our accounts and forestall a greater retribution.

On Yom Kippur, we say in our prayers, "Behold, I stand before You like a vessel full of shame and disgrace. Wipe them away in Your great kindness, but not through suffering." The Shelah, at the end of *Meseches Yoma*, is puzzled by this prayer. How does this work? If a person did an *aveirah*, he has to pay, he has to suffer. How then can we ask to be exempt from suffering? The answer, says the Shelah, is that we are begging Hashem to accept those disappointments, those insults, those snide remarks in lieu of suffering. Let all those small doses of indignity that add up until we are like a vessel full of shame and disgrace, let them all be counted for us as an expiation of our sins so that we should not have to suffer any more.

Let me tell you a story about Napoleon. In 1812, the French army besieged Moscow. The Russian army defended the city tenaciously, and the siege dragged on for a very long time. The dreaded Russian winter was fast approaching, and the French troops were becoming demoralized. Many officers advised Napoleon to abandon the siege and withdraw.

"What you're saying has merit," Napoleon admitted, "but I want to give it one more chance. I want to find out the level of morale among the Russian soldiers. Then I'll make my decision."

But how were they to gauge the level of Russian morale? The only way was to see for themselves. So Napoleon and several hand-picked officers disguised themselves as Russian peasants and entered the city.

Where do you find out what the Russian soldier is thinking? In a tavern, of course. So they followed some soldiers into a tavern and settled down to listen. It didn't take long before the soldiers were grumbling and complaining that they were starving. They all agreed that they might as well surrender. Elated, Napoleon and his companions got up to leave.

Suddenly, one of the soldiers glanced at Napoleon and jumped to his feet.

"Comrades!" he cried. "That's Napoleon."

The others laughed. "Sit down, Boris. You've had too much vodka."

"It is, I tell you. I've been to France. I saw him. That's Napoleon."

"It can't be," they insisted. "The emperor of France? In a Russian tavern? You must be out of your mind. How can that be Napoleon?"

While the soldiers argued among themselves, Napoleon and his companions quickly devised a plan.

"Hey, Sasha," one of his companions said to Napoleon.

Napoleon brought a drink, but in his feigned clumsiness, he spilled it all over the man's shirt. The man let out a cry of rage and slapped Napoleon across the face, shouting, "You clumsy oaf, take that!" Napoleon fell to the ground, and the man started kicking him.

Meanwhile, the spectacle had caught the attention of the Russian soldiers.

"Look, Boris," one of them shouted. "There's your Napoleon. He's getting kicked around. C'mon, is that how they treat an emperor? Maybe you should go to his rescue."

With that, the soldiers lost interest in Napoleon, and he and his companions were able to slip away.

When they returned to the French encampment, the officer who had slapped Napoleon fell to his knees. "I beg you for forgiveness," he pleaded. "Will you please forgive me?"

"Forgive you?" said Napoleon. "I owe my life to you. Those slaps and kicks saved me!"

The same applies to us. The slaps and kicks can save us. Most of us, unfortunately, are not like the Klausenberger Rav and his people in the camps to whom the *ashamnus* and the *al cheits* do not apply. Unfortunately, they do apply to us, and we can use all the help we can get. Those insults we suffer can help us. Those insults we suffer can sometimes save our lives.

But here we come to a very crucial point. It is not only the insults themselves. It is the way we deal with them. The Almighty gave us a secret weapon.

He gave us two words that can absolve us of all our sins: two words that can save us, two simple words. What are those two words?

"I forgive."

Not "I'm sorry," Not "I ask forgiveness." No. I forgive others, no matter who they may be. I forgive my wife, my husband, my son, my daughter, my neighbor, my employer, my rabbi, my friend, my enemy. I forgive.

Our Sages tells us, "If someone lets things pass without insisting on his rights, all his sins are forgiven." If a person is magnanimous and forgiving with others, Hashem treats him in the same way. That's how the relationship works.

One Erev Yom Kippur, two people were having a heated conversation in Rav Zalman Volozhiner's *shul*.

"I know I did you wrong," one of them said to the other. "But I'm asking you to forgive me. Please forgive me."

"Absolutely not," said the other. "Even though it's Erev Yom Kippur, I will not forgive you. You slandered me and ruined my reputation. The Torah doesn't require me to forgive you, and I won't."

Rav Zalman Volozhiner, who was standing nearby, heard

the exchange and called over the offended party. "Let me ask you a question," he said. "The Gemara says that Jerusalem was destroyed because people insisted on adhering to the letter of the law. Because people insisted on the exact letter of the law, they refused to bend or give an inch. They insisted on their full rights. But what does this mean? Doesn't the Prophet tell us that it was destroyed because of the prevalence of idolatry, bloodshed and adultery? I'll tell you what it means. If the people in Jerusalem had been willing to forgive each other, then the Almighty would have forgiven them even for the horrendous sins of idolatry, bloodshed and adultery. What caused the downfall of Jerusalem? Its people's refusal to forgive."

Two Jews with the identical record can come before the Heavenly Court, and they can receive entirely different judgments. Hashem may forgive one and grant him a good year, while He punishes the other one severely. How can this be? The one who is willing to forgive will be himself forgiven. Our Sages told us so. We can take it to the bank.

Forgiving other people, that is the key. Not just a grudging forgiveness. True forgiveness emanates from a generosity of spirit, an attitude of magnanimity. That is what Hashem wants to see from us.

I once heard a story about a young couple in *Eretz Yisrael* who didn't have children for years and years. They tried all sorts of *eitzos* and *segulos*, but nothing worked.

One time, the husband, who learned in a Litvishe *yeshivah*, went to visit a *Chassidishe rebbe* in Bnei Brak who was known to work wonders for people who didn't have children. The *rebbe* invited the young man to come for Rosh Hashanah. It was well-known that whoever got Maftir on the first day of Rosh Hashanah in this *rebbe's shul* would be blessed with a child.

Before Rosh Hashanah, the young couple traveled from Jerusalem to Bnei Brak. They were excited but very apprehensive. They had waited so long. Would this finally be the answer to their prayers?

After Maariv on the first night of Rosh Hashanah, while everyone was exchanging greetings and good wishes, the young man noticed a man standing in the back of the *shul* who seemed somewhat out of place. He walked over to wish the stranger a good Yom Tov and struck up a conversation.

"So tell me," he said, "is this your regular *shul?*"

"Oh, no," said the stranger. "I never come here, but I came for a special reason." He looked embarrassed for a moment but also happy to share his thoughts with someone else. "You see, my wife and I don't have any children, and I heard that if you get Maftir here on the first day of Rosh Hashanah it can help." He shrugged. "So here I am. I thought maybe I could ask them for Maftir and see if it does any good."

When the young man heard these words, he immediately decided that he would step aside and allow the other man to get Maftir. In fact, he wouldn't even come to the *shul* the next day so as to present no conflict.

I don't know the entire end to the story. I don't know if the man who got Maftir had a child. But I do know that the young man who forfeited his right to the Maftir was blessed with a baby that year.

Rav Chaim Shmulevitz, the Rosh Yeshivah of the Mirrer Yeshivah, used to talk about his most vivid recollection of the Six-Day War. It took place in the air-raid shelter under the *yeshivah*.

As soon as the air-raid siren sounded, everyone ran for the shelter, not only the *talmidim* of the *yeshivah* but everyone in the whole neighborhood. The bombs started falling, and they could hear the dull thud of the explosions. All of a sudden, there was a tremendous roar and the entire shelter shook. One bomb had come very close to the building. A moment later, there was another.

People started screaming and praying. Some people shouted, *"Shema Yisrael!"*

Among the people in the shelter was an embittered woman who was known as the neighborhood *agunah*. Her husband had left her but refused to divorce her properly. This woman therefore lived in limbo, not married and not single. An angry, tormented woman.

At that moment, when the bombs started falling right above their heads, this woman stood up and declared, "Hashem, You know that my husband made my life miserable. He made my life a prison. I have no present, no future. Hashem, I forgive my husband. Won't you forgive the Jewish people? Won't you forgive us and save us?"

"It wasn't the *talmidim* in the *yeshivah* that saved us that night," said Rav Chaim Shmulevitz. "It was that woman. Because that woman was ready to forgive, we were all forgiven."

That's the key to *teshuvah*. I forgive you. And perhaps that was what the Rebbe Reb Elimelech admired about the *kaparos* of the innkeeper in the village. *Kaparah* begins with forgiveness.

A Nation of Lions

J UST AS SPRINGTIME IS IN THE AIR WHEN APRIL COMES around, *teshuvah* is in the air when the month of Elul comes around. But there is a broad gap between being in the air to entering our hearts, and all too often, *teshuvah* doesn't make it all the way in. What exactly is the problem? Why do we have such difficulty doing *teshuvah*?

One of the answers I hear from people is that they just find it hard to get into the mood. Caught up in the hustle and bustle of their hectic schedules, some people find it rather difficult to get into the proper frame of mind to do *teshuvah*. Before they know it, they have swept through Rosh Hashanah and Yom Kippur without really having the opportunity to really get into it.

This apparently was not a major problem for earlier generations. They didn't need any special ambiance or background music to get into the mood. They were aware of the stark reality of these days. They knew what an Elul meant. They knew what the *Aseres Yemei Teshuvah* are all about. They knew what was at stake. They had no trouble with moods.

Before World War II, a *rav* in a town in Germany announced that the first Selichos would be said on Sunday at 4 o'clock in the morning. The *rav* lived in an apartment over the *shul*, and during the night before Selichos he heard rustling in the *shul*. He looked at the clock. Two o'clock. Who would be in the *shul* at 2 o'clock in the morning? Surely, it was an intruder.

His heart pounding wildly, the *rav* grabbed a robe and crept down the stairs to investigate. To his amazement, and immense relief, he saw one of his older congregants sitting in his seat.

"What are you doing here in the middle of the night?" the *rav* asked. "Why don't you go to sleep?"

"Sleep?" said the man. "Who can sleep at a time like this?"

This man, who lived in the 20th century, was an ordinary Jew, not a famous *tzaddik*. But he had no problem getting into the mood. He knew what Elul is. He knew what the *Aseres Yemei Teshuvah* are.

Several years ago I spent Shabbos in my hometown of Seattle two weeks before Rosh Hashanah. I came into the *shul* Friday night, and not one but two elderly Jews, one of whom had been with the Mirrer Yeshivah in Shanghai, asked me why I was in Seattle during Elul and not in my *yeshivah*. These people and others like them appreciated the value of Elul. The people of their generation apparently had no trouble with moods. People in our generation have trouble with moods.

So how do we get into the mood? If we take the blinders off our eyes and face reality, we can get into the mood very quickly.

Rav Chaim Friedlander, *mashgiach* of the Ponevezh Yeshivah in *Eretz Yisrael*, once wrote a letter to his *talmidim* during the month of Elul. At the time, he was in Sloan-Kettering Memorial Hospital in New York City undergoing treatment for the cancer which eventually took his life.

"The Gemara (*Rosh Hashanah* 16b) tells us," he writes, "that a year that begins with poverty will ultimately be enriched. What does this mean? Rashi explains that when Jewish people see themselves as impoverished on Rosh Hashanah they will enjoy a year rich with blessings. If they approach the Day of Judgment with humility and trepidation, if they feel destitute, if they feel like people who have nothing, they will be successful."

In modern accounting, there is a term called zero-based budgeting. You have to get funding for your agency or department for every new fiscal year. You don't come with any givens, with any assumptions whatsoever. Every line on that budget has to be justified as if it was never submitted before.

That is Rosh Hashanah — zero-based budgeting. That is how we have to come into Rosh Hashanah. We have nothing.

Nothing? we might ask. We have nothing? But that's not accurate. We have our families, our friends, our health, our skills, our homes, our investments.

Thinking this way is all a mistake. We really do have nothing. We do not have squatters' rights to all the blessings Hashem has granted us in His great kindness. He is under no obligation to extend our blessings for another year. We really do have nothing when we come before the Heavenly Court on the Day of Judgment, and only if we realize this can we expect to gain a favorable judgment.

"I had the opportunity," writes Rav Friedlander, "to experience the grace of the Almighty, the One Who delivers from death and grants new life. I'm a living example of what it means to feel destitute on the Day of Judgment. A person may think he is secure in his health, but it is only a mirage. His life always hangs by a thread."

The Torah tells us that on the last day of his life "*Vayeilech Moshe.* Moshe went." The *Midrash Tanchuma* explains that this phrase implies a sharp rebuke to the Jewish people. Where is the rebuke? If we look into the text, we find no words of rebuke, no reproach.

The *Yalkut,* however, discerns a frightening rebuke in the very next *passuk.* "I am one hundred and twenty years old today," Moshe tells the Jewish people. "I can no longer come and go." The people were astonished. How could this be? Only the day before he was able to soar to the heavens like an eagle, and today, he can't even cross the river like everyone else. What happened to Moshe? "For Hashem said to me, 'You will not cross this Jordan River.'"

This was the rebuke. These were the words of admonition. You cannot take anything for granted. Today you can fly like an eagle, tomorrow you may not be able to walk. All is in Hashem's hands.

People who understand this, people who realize that everything, absolutely everything is on the line on Rosh Hashanah, act differently. People who know that their lives hang in the balance act differently.

I remember the time when my young son was scheduled for extremely delicate surgery. I remember that day vividly. It is the kind of day which is never forgotten. We came to the hospital, my wife, my son and I, early in the morning. The hospital was quiet, and we waited in a room with other patients scheduled for surgery.

I remember a woman there sitting with her daughter. The little girl clutched a teddy bear, while her mother spoke to her gently. There were other families in the quiet waiting room, all acting normally.

The wheels of the process began to move. The patients were taken away for surgery, and the families were told to go to a waiting room on a different floor. When we arrived, I again saw the mother of the little girl who had been clutching the teddy bear. This time she did not seem so normal and relaxed. She was sitting there and weeping. Another woman in the room was near hysteria, and two friends were trying desperately to calm her down.

These people knew what was hanging in the balance. They knew what it meant to feel destitute. They were taking nothing for granted. When the messages from the operating rooms came in, they would pounce on the words and try to dissect them for their last ounce of meaning. Did the doctor say it's going well? Or very well? Did he look nervous? Did he look concerned? Did he try to avert his eyes?

I remember thinking to myself that my wife and I were fortunate that we could say *Tehillim*, that we could turn to our loving Father in Heaven for comfort and encouragement.

There was one family in that room whose behavior was bizarre. The patient they were waiting for was having open heart surgery. What did these people do? They were putting together a thousand-piece puzzle. I'm not faulting these people. I remember wondering if perhaps the puzzle was a defense mechanism or a distraction. I also remember wondering how Hashem views people who are busy during the *Aseres Yemei Teshuvah* fooling around with thousand-piece puzzles and other such nonsense.

If we only gave more thought to the fragility of life, we would be better prepared for the Day of Judgment. If only we thought about what we have riding on the line, we would have no trouble getting in the mood for *teshuvah*.

Let me tell you about one of the shortest yet most powerful *teshuvah drashos* ever given. It consisted of nine words.

Around the turn of the century, the Jewish community of New York City appointed its first and only chief rabbi. The committee went all the way to Vilna to invite a man of great Torah erudition and impeccable credentials, a man who could keep an audience spellbound for hours, quoting verbatim extensively from the sources without the benefit of an open text. This man was the famous Rav Yaakov Yosef, in whose honor the famous Rabbi Yaakov Yosef Yeshivah, otherwise known as RJJ, was named. Rav Yaakov Yosef's addresses to the congregation on *Shabbos Shuvah* were among the highlights of Jewish life in New York City. People would pack the *shul* to hear the great rabbi's words of inspiration.

One year, Rav Yaakov Yosef suffered a stroke, and his speech and motor abilities were affected. People wondered whether he would be able to speak in public on *Shabbos Shuvah*. It seemed doubtful, but Rav Yaakov Yosef was determined. He did, however, make a concession to his stroke. He would quote from open texts rather than from memory.

The announcement that he would be speaking after all caused a sensation in the city. People come from near and far to Manhattan for that *Shabbos Shuvah* for what promised to be a historic occasion. On Shabbos, there was not even an extra inch of standing room in the Great Synagogue on the Lower East Side, and the crowd overflowed onto Norfolk Street.

Slowly and laboriously, Rav Yaakov Yosef made his way to the pulpit, and he started to speak.

He began, "The Gemara says — "

Silence.

Once again, he attempted to speak, "The Gemara says —"

Silence again.

A third time, "The Gemara says — "

Again, the same result.

In bitter frustration, Rav Yaakov Yosef broke down and cried. Nine words were all he had managed to get out, and he couldn't go on.

"I had everything prepared," he told the people around him, "but I can't even remember what the subject was."

How terribly tragic. Here was this celebrated rabbi, the pride and joy of the entire Jewish community of New York City, and he couldn't say more than nine pathetic words. He couldn't even remember the subject he had chosen to discuss.

How shaken the people must have been after witnessing this sad spectacle. What guarantees were there in life? Yesterday, the man had soared like an eagle, but now he couldn't even take a simple step. What a powerful *teshuvah* message that must have been for everyone present.

Everything is on the line. Everything. Those people most probably had no trouble getting in the mood.

Beside the mood issue, however, there is also a second problem people commonly encounter when they consider *teshuvah*. "How much is my *teshuvah* worth?" one man once told me. "Let's not kid ourselves. This is not my first Yom Kippur. I've been down this road before. I've gone through the process, I've said I'm going to be better, I made resolutions, I tried to improve my life. But I'm still basically the same person I was last year. So what's the use?"

The man has a point. This is a feeling that's been troubling Jews for thousands of years.

Over 2,000 years ago, during the Babylonian exile, the prophet Yechezkel spoke of this ambivalence towards *teshuvah*.

"We are pining away with the same sins," the Jewish people had complained. "How can we return when we still have the same old sins?"

"Tell them," Hashem said to Yechezkel, "to do *teshuvah*. I do not want the sinful to perish, only to repent and live on."

Do *teshuvah*, says Hashem. *Teshuvah* helps. *Teshuvah* itself contains the antidote to these poisonous feelings, for it is based on two fundamental principles that negate them.

The first principle of *teshuvah* is that people have the capacity to change. We can grow. We can become better. This is the very essence of the *Aseres Yemei Teshuvah*.

The Midrash offers us an incredible insight into the *Aseres Yemei Teshuvah*. To what do we owe this great gift called *Aseres Yemei Teshuvah*? It is in the merit of the 10 *nisyonos*, explains the Midrash, the ten ordeals by which Hashem tested Avraham Avinu and found him faithful. It is also in the merit of Avraham Avinu's pleading with Hashem to spare Sedom from destruction if only 10 righteous people could be found there.

Clearly, *Aseres Yemei Teshuvah* works on two distinct levels. On the one hand, it is a transcendent opportunity for spectacular growth. It is a time when all of us in our own way can reenact the climb of Avraham Avinu, rising step by step to new levels of spirituality. It is a time when the great can become greater, the pure can become purer; they can become sublime.

But what about the rest of us? What about ordinary, well-meaning people who struggle daily to maintain basic levels of spirituality? What about those of us that slip, slide and stumble through the year? What about those of us whose eyes are not on the spiritual peaks we hope to scale but on the spiritual abyss we hope to avoid? What did our forefather Avraham bequeath to us?

Here we encounter the second aspect of the *Aseres Yemei Teshuvah*, the critical aspect for most of us. We can do *teshuvah*, we can change. In fact, anyone can change, as Avraham Avinu so aptly demonstrated when he pleaded for the corrupt people of Sedom. Sedom was a wicked, rotten city, a city of despicable villains. Nonetheless, Avraham Avinu begged Hashem, "Won't you spare this city if only 50 righteous people can be found there? Forty? Thirty? Ten?"

People have an unbelievable capacity to change, Avraham Avinu was saying. No matter how low they sink, they can rise again. If there is the least spark of decency left in Sedom, it should not be destroyed. Even 10 righteous people can change a whole city, because people can change. And Hashem consented to his argument.

That is what *Aseres Yemei Teshuvah* is all about. Don't give up. You can change. You can become better. This is the first principle of *teshuvah*.

There is also a second principle of *teshuvah* which contends that people are resilient. We can get up. Even if we fall, we can still get up. We can pick ourselves up, dust ourselves off and start all over again. As Shlomo Hamelech tells us in his stellar wisdom (*Mishlei* 24:16), "*Sheva yipol tzaddik vekam.* A tzaddik can fall seven times and still rise." Do you know what a *tzaddik* is? A *tzaddik* is not necessarily a person that doesn't do an *aveirah*. A *tzaddik* is a person who falls again and again but gets up each time.

A *talmid* of Rav Yitzchak Hutner once wrote to him about his frustrations in the spiritual realm, "I'm tired. I try so hard, but I don't see myself getting any better. I don't see growth. It's such a difficult struggle."

"Never give up," Rav Hutner wrote back, "*Sheva yipol tzaddik vekam*. That's what it's all about. The battles, the struggles, that's a *tzaddik*. What do you think the *passuk* means? That a *tzaddik* gets up even though he falls? That misses the entire point. The true intent of Shlomo Hamelech is to teach us that the way to rise is through repeated falls. You become a *tzaddik* by falling down and rising. You grow from the experience and become a better person. Growth comes from struggle. It is not automatic. You can't coast and grow. You've got to fight to grow. You've got to struggle to grow. You may lose the battles. You may fight and lose them. But you can win the war. You can become bigger by the falls, by the foibles, by the stumbling. That is the road to becoming a *tzaddik*. We can grow from our struggles."

In his letter, Rav Hutner goes on to bemoan the popular biographies of *gedolim* that portray them as perfect people from the womb. The typical *gadol* about whom our children read washed *negel vasser* on his own when he was 1 year old. He knew Mishnayos when he was 6. He never fought with his brothers and sisters. He knew the entire Shas by age 13, wrote a brilliant *sefer* by 20 and was a *tzaddik* every moment of his entire life. So what's the reaction of the reader? This is not a human being. This is an angel. It's an interesting story, but what does it have to do with me? But that's not how one becomes a *tzaddik*. That's not who our *gedolim* were. They were very human, they were very normal, and they had their battles and they had their struggles. They persevered and emerged victorious.

It is not my intent, of course, to discourage people from giving these books to their children. When I was growing up in America, the only biographies available for children in the English language were about people like Lou Gehrig and Amelia Earhart. How blessed we are that today we can give our children biographies of *tzaddikim* and *gedolim*. But how much more blessed we would be if these biographies would convey the struggles that made them *tzaddikim*. How much better if they would demonstrate that each and every one of our children can rise without limit if they undertake the struggle with courage and determination.

The entire world stands in awe of the Chafetz Chaim, of his *tzidkus* and his battle against *lashon hara*. Did the Chafetz Chaim ever speak *lashon hara*? Probably never, we think, and certainly not after his *bar mitzvah*.

But can we really be certain about this? This is the delicate question Rav Hutner poses in that same letter. "Who can possibly know," he writes, "about all the battles, the struggles, the pitfalls, the failures and the setbacks the Chafetz Chaim experienced in his battle against *lashon hara*?"

It certainly wasn't easy. The Chafetz Chaim, just like the rest of us, had a *yetzer hara*, and he undoubtedly had to struggle against it. He may have fallen, but he got up again. He never gave up. He never threw up his hands on Erev Yom Kippur and told himself he was no better than before. He was a relentless fighter who never accepted defeat.

"And those who are lost in the land of Ashur will come," prophesied Yeshayahu about Messianic times, "and those who are displaced in the land of Egypt." That is the final *teshuvah*. Those lost in Ashur and those displaced in Egypt will come back and do *teshuvah*.

Who is farther removed, one who is "lost" or one who is "displaced"? asks Rav Tzaddok HaKohen. Surely, the one who is lost is farther removed. Why then does he return before the one who is merely displaced?

We have to understand the difference, explains Rav Tzaddok HaKohen, between the land of Ashur and the land of Egypt. Ashur was a country of rocky, semi-arid hills where farmers had to struggle and scrape to bring forth the bounty of the land. But Egypt was a breadbasket. You planted in the rich loam, the Nile River overflowed, and you harvested.

If you are lost in the land of Ashur, declares the Prophet, if your life has been a spiritual struggle, if it has been a spiritual battle, if you've had to fight your *yetzer hara*, it will be easier to bring you back, even if you lost the battle. But if you were in the land of Egypt, if you did not struggle against the *yetzer hara*, it will be harder to bring you back, even if you were only displaced.

Rav Levi Yitzchak of Berditchev once said that we have to learn three things from a little child. When something hurts a little child, he cries out to his father. A little child is always occupied, always busy, never idle. And when a little child falls, he always gets up. If you fall, you get up. That is one of the most critical lessons of life. You cannot allow yourself to remain down. This resilience, this capacity to fall and rise again is a hallmark of our people. We are a nation that gets up. No matter how much we are pushed down, we get back up. We are "a nation of survivors" (*Yirmiyahu* 31:1).

The Gemara (*Berachos* 12b) tells us that our Sages wanted to incorporate the story of Balak in our daily *Shema* because it contains Bilam's description of the Jewish people as lions. The Sfas Emes explains that this is our defining characteristic. We are a nation that gets up. We are a nation that fights valiantly like lions.

The *Midrash Tanchuma* glories in the resilience of the Jewish people. Even if they are spiritually asleep, even if they go for years without *mitzvos*, they can rise again like lions. A person does an *aveirah*, says the Midrash, and what is his reaction? He does *teshuvah* and accepts upon himself the Kingship of the Holy One, Blessed is He. We are like undaunted lions. A nation that gets up, that is never beaten. A nation of survivors. This is the quality that has kept us going through thousands of years of exile.

In 1492, the Edict of Expulsion was issued against the

Jews of Spain. Either they would convert to Christianity or leave. The Chassid Yavetz, a great *gadol* who lived through this dreadful period, wrote about some of the Jewish experiences of the time. One man sold all his belongings for a small fraction of their worth. With the money he realized from the sale, he hired a boat to take him and his family to Italy. The boat captain dumped the man and his family on a remote island in the Mediterranean and left them to die. The man's entire family did indeed perish from disease and exposure to the elements, and he alone survived. How did he react? "Hashem!" the man cried out, "You are trying to push me away, but I won't go. I'm going to stay with You regardless." Like a lion. We are a people that rises like a lion.

In the terrible years of Tach v'Tat (1648-9), the Cossacks slaughtered one third of European Jewry. At the funeral of his own son many centuries later, the Chafetz Chaim spoke about one particular woman who had lost her husband and son. How did she react? What did she say? "Hashem!" she cried out. "Until now You and my family shared my love. But now, You alone possess all my love." Incredible. This is a nation that doesn't give up. This is a nation that arises from the ashes.

There is no doubt in my mind that the average Bais Yaakov graduate is far more knowledgeable than that courageous Jewish woman. It would not surprise me if that woman didn't even know how to read a *passuk* in the *Chumash*. But she knew what being Jewish is all about. She knew that she could not allow herself to remain down. She knew the meaning of resilience. She knew how to rise from the depths of despair.

In our own lifetime, who needs more evidence than the survivors of the Holocaust who went through the most abysmal hell and emerged to rebuild a glorious Jewish nation? Our own fathers and mothers, grandfathers and grandmothers, uncles and aunts, who saw everything dear to them destroyed before their very eyes and still stand tall in their pride as Jews. Like lions.

In his memoir of the Adolf Eichmann trial, Israeli prosecutor Gideon Hausner writes that Eichmann hung a velvet *paroches* from an *aron kodesh* on the entrance to the gas chamber in the Treblinka concentration camp. Embroidered on the *paroches* were the words "*Zeh hashaar Lashem, tzaddikim yavo'u vo.*" This is the gate for the righteous! It is beyond imagination that people had to go to their deaths faced with this mockery of Hashem and humanity.

But you know what? We took back the *paroches*! The Jewish people are still here. We got up. We never gave up. We rose again like lions. That is the hallmark of the Jewish people. That is what we are all about.

Have we fallen?

Yes.

Are we as good as we want to be?

No.

But that's the message of *teshuvah*. Don't give up. Lose the battle, but win the war. Like lions.

During the *Aseres Yemei Teshuvah*, as we sit down to take stock of our lives, we all want to improve, to be better spouses, better children to our parents, better parents to our children, better friends, better people. Let us do something concrete about it. Let us take even a small step. Let us win even a small battle.

How many books have we read about child rearing? How many lectures have we heard? Let us make it concrete. No more calling the children names. To undertake to stop yelling may be too much, because we're going to fall down. Just no more name-calling. I once heard about a girl who thought her name was Klutz until her teacher set her straight at age 7. So let's not call our children names. A small victory. But concrete. Be better. Get up. Do something.

Sure, we'd like to say we won't speak any more *lashon hara*. But that may be too much to expect. But how about no *lashon hara* one day a week? Just one day. How about no *lashon hara* on Shabbos? Imagine what an improvement that would be, two birds with one stone. One day less *lashon hara*, and practically no more talking in *shul* on Shabbos.

Think about a typical secular Jew who considers becoming religious but is intimidated by the prospect. "Rabbi, what should I do?" he says. "I just can't keep kosher all the time. Maybe I can keep kosher at home, but not when I'm out in the business world."

So what does the rabbi tell him? Forget it, it's all or nothing? Of course not. You do what you can. You start with a small step and continue one step at a time. You grow. You may fall, but you get up.

Do something concrete. Review your *tzedakah* practices. Are you really giving enough? Perhaps you can forgo one or two luxuries and give some more *tzedakah*. Perhaps you can cut your vacation short by one day and give that money to *tzedakah*. Perhaps you can go out to eat one less time a month and give that money to *tzedakah*. Perhaps you can give this money to the schools your children attend over and above the tuition you are already paying. Perhaps if people would do this, we would be able to pay *rebbeim* decent wages. After all, why shouldn't a *rebbi* make as much as a lawyer or an accountant? Is he any less professional? Is his work any less important?

Do something concrete. Win. Get up.

Review your Torah learning habits. Of course, it's a struggle. How many *sedarim* have we all started and broken? But don't give up. If you can't see yourself learning Gemara, let it be *Tanach*. Let it be Halachah. Stay for the *rav's* five-minute *shiur* after Shacharis every morning. Do something, anything, as long as you bring more Torah into your life.

Change. Get up. You can be better. That's the lesson of *teshuvah*. Human beings can change. There are going to be battles. There are going to be struggles. There are going to be losses. There are going to be regressions. But get up.

Teshuvah is the overriding theme of Jewish history. We are a nation of survivors. We are a nation that gets up. We are a nation of lions.

The Pursuit of
Happiness

AN OLD QUESTION ABOUT ROSH HASHANAH AND YOM
Kippur has troubled the commentators for hundreds
of years. Since Rosh Hashanah is the Day of
Judgment and Yom Kippur the Day of Atonement, wouldn't
it be more appropriate for Rosh Hashanah to be preceded by
Yom Kippur rather than to be followed by it? Wouldn't it be
better to pass through a process of atonement before we are
summoned to a Day of Judgment?

Many solutions are offered to this question, but the general consensus seems to be that we cannot expect to enter
Yom Kippur with the proper frame of mind unless we first
experience Rosh Hashanah. Before we can approach the
task of doing *teshuvah* with utmost seriousness on Yom
Kippur, we must first feel the dread of *eimas hadin*, the awe

of pending judgment, on Rosh Hashanah. Only after we have reaffirmed deep in our consciousness that the Almighty is the King, and that we are all His servants, can we even hope to do real *teshuvah*.

In times gone by, this was what Rosh Hashanah used to accomplish for people. It filled their hearts with an awestruck awareness of Hashem as King over every last corner of the entire Universe.

Rav Aharon Karliner, one of the great Chassidic luminaries, would wait anxiously for the *chazzan* to say the word *HaMelech*, the King, during Shacharis on Rosh Hashanah. One year, he fainted and fell to the ground as soon as he heard the word.

Why did he faint when he heard the word *HaMelech*? What thoughts passed through his mind?

Before we discuss the exalted thoughts of Rav Aharon Karliner, however, let us ask ourselves a different, somewhat troubling question. What thoughts pass through *our* minds when we hear the word *HaMelech*? Do we wonder who the *chazzan* is? Do we listen critically to determine if he is singing on key? Those were most definitely not the thoughts that Rav Aharon Karliner was thinking.

Rav Aharon Karliner, as he later told his *chassidim*, was reminded of a Gemara *(Gittin 56a)*. When Jerusalem was besieged by the Roman armies led by the general Vespasian, Rav Yochanan ben Zakkai feigned death and escaped the city in a coffin. He then made his way to the Roman encampment and appeared before Vespasian to plead for concessions which would ensure the future of the Jewish people.

"Greetings, O king," he said to Vespasian, thereby predicting the general's imminent ascension to the imperial throne. Shortly thereafter, the news arrived that the Roman Senate had indeed elected him emperor.

"You deserve a punishment," Vespasian replied. "If you truly consider me a king, why haven't you come earlier?"

Said Rav Aharon Karliner, "When I heard the word

HaMelech, I recalled the words of the Roman emperor, 'If you truly consider me a king, why haven't you come earlier?' And I said to myself, If I truly considered Hashem to be our King, our *Melech*, then why didn't I do *teshuvah* earlier? Why has it taken me so long to appear before the *Melech*?"

The thought was so frightening to him that he fainted. This is true *eimas hadin*. This was a man who truly trembled at the prospect of judgment before the Heavenly Court.

In this generation, there were also people who had *eimas hadin*. I once saw Rav Yaakov Ruderman come into the *beis midrash* on Erev Rosh Hashanah to address the *talmidim* of the *yeshivah*. "Today is the last day of the year," he began. "Tomorrow is Rosh Hashanah!" Then he burst into uncontrollable weeping and couldn't go on. That was *eimas hadin*. That is how people used to go into Rosh Hashanah. That is what inspired them to *teshuvah*.

However, there is also another avenue by which we can approach *teshuvah*. The Torah tells us that Rosh Hashanah is a *Yom Teruah*, a day of resonant sounds. Our Sages tell us *teruah* refers to *yevavah*, a wailing sound. What is considered a wailing sound? The sound Sisera's mother made when she saw her son go off to battle is called a *yevavah*. She stood by the window, and she cried, "When is my son Sisra going to come back from war?" We also find a *Tosefos* which states that the reason we sound the *shofar* 100 times is to recall the 100 cries of Sisra's mother.

What is the meaning of this? Why do our Sages want to remind us about Sisra's mother on Rosh Hashanah? What is so meaningful about her cries?

Rav Yitzchak Blazer, a great *baal mussar,* explains that Sisra's mother was in a turmoil when she looked out from her window and saw her son go off to battle. On the one hand, this could be the greatest moment of his entire career. He could come back victorious and covered with glory. But on the other hand, he could come back in a coffin. The battle might end in disaster, and he could perish in disgrace. Which would it be? The pendulum of her emotions swung from one end to the other, and she cried out in anguish.

That is what Rosh Hashanah is all about, says Rav Yitzchak Blazer. That is the kind of turmoil that should be raging inside our own hearts. What will this day bring? Will it bring us great success? Will it bring us health and joy and prosperity? Will this year be a crowning glory for us? Or will it bring dreaded consequences, Heaven forbid? Will this year bring us up or will it bring us down?

These are the thoughts and feelings our Sages wanted to inspire by reminding us of Sisra's mother, and there are definitely times during the day when we feel it strongly. Most probably, it hits us during *Unesaneh Tokef*, when we come face to face with our mortality. Who will live, we say, and who will die. Who will live to enjoy serenity, and who will be confounded. But does this realization last?

There is yet another way our Sages sought to inspire us to do *teshuvah*. The Gemara (*Shabbos* 153a) advises a person to do *teshuvah* one day before his death. Therefore, since a person does not know when he will die, he must do *teshuvah* every day.

Rav Mordechai Gifter reads a deeper message into these words of the Sages. Philosophers have pointed out that contrast is very important to accurate evaluation. In order to appreciate the gift of good health we have to take a long, hard look at the harrowing aspects of illness. Life, therefore, can sometimes best be savored in the shadow of death. If we contemplate the fleeting, flimsy nature of this thing called life, we realize how exceedingly precious it is and how preposterous it would be to fritter it away on nonsense. And so we are inspired to do *teshuvah*, to give everlasting meaning to every moment of this precious life by imbuing it with Torah, with *mitzvos*, with spirituality. This message is implicit in the words of our Sages. Think about the day you will die and you will be energized to live. And what is life, real life, without *teshuvah*?

Let us take a closer look at how the gift of life depends on *teshuvah*.

In America, the Declaration of Independence has established three inalienable rights for the individual. They are life, liberty and the pursuit of happiness. That last phrase, the pursuit of happiness, is truly a stroke of genius. No other phrase encapsulates what motivates all people than does this phrase. Everyone wants happiness. Everyone pursues it. People spend all their days and years pursuing this elusive matter of happiness. They devote all their waking hours and all their ingenuity and creativity attempting to discover happiness. But do they succeed? After all, what is happiness? How do people define happiness? How do our Sages define happiness?

The *Navi* tells us (*Melachim I* 8:65) that when King Solomon inaugurated the *Beis Hamikdash* there was a great celebration. All of Israel came together from border to border for the festivities in one great outburst of joy. After the festival was over, they all "returned to their homes, happy and content."

The *Yalkut Shimoni* explains that "happy" implies that they delighted in the radiance of the Divine Presence.

Rav Avraham Pam raises an interesting question. How did the Sages know that "happy" refers to delight in the radiance of the Divine Presence? Elsewhere, the Sages tells us that wine and meat bring happiness. If so, perhaps this happiness as well derived from wine and meat. How do the Sages know that it derived from a spiritual encounter with Hashem?

The answer, explains Rav Pam, is that this happiness could not possibly have derived from wine and meat. The *Navi* tells us that all went home happy, those who lived in the far reaches of the country as well as those who lived nearby. Now, although those who lived nearby might have reached home in a matter of hours, those people who lived in the outlying districts undoubtedly endured journeys lasting many days. How then can we be told with such assurance that they all reached home happy? Maybe time and the travails of the road dissipated the happiness of those who had to travel great distances.

Clearly then, this happiness was not of a physical nature. Physical happiness does not linger on. It quickly becomes a memory, and quickly after that, the memory fades away. By the time they arrived home a week or two later, any happiness they derived from wine and meat would surely have been long forgotten. The only happiness that is enduring, the only happiness that does not fade with the passage of time, is happiness of a spiritual nature. Our Sages, therefore, understood without question that their happiness derived from an encounter with the Divine Presence.

We try to pursue happiness. We're looking for that elusive good time. We think we will find happiness by letting the good times roll. We think we will find happiness in money. We think we will find happiness in vacations. We think all sorts of things will help us find this elusive pot at the end of the rainbow called happiness.

But it is all futile. Only one road leads to true happiness. Only one delivers lasting happiness, and that is *ruchnius*, spirituality. The more spirituality we introduce into our lives, the happier and more content we will be.

Paradoxically, however, we are inclined to resist spirituality, because we don't want to infringe on our happiness. We are afraid that if we become more religious, if we learn more Torah, if we do more *mitzvos*, we will restrict our lives and our prospects for happiness. But the exact opposite is true. The more spirituality we bring into our lives, the more Torah, the more *mitzvos*, the more *chessed*, the more *tzedakah*, the happier we will become. That's the only kind of happiness that lasts.

The Rambam in *Hilchos Teshuvah* finds an important symbolism in the sounding of the *shofar* on Rosh Hashanah. The *shofar* calls out to the dreamers, "Wake up from your slumber!" This is an unusual phrase for the Rambam, and indeed, there is only one other place where the Rambam speaks of a figurative awakening of the slumberer.

The Rambam writes in *Hilchos Mezuzah*, "A person is obligated to be scrupulous regarding the *mitzvah* of *mezuzah*, because it is a universal and constant obligation. With this *mitzvah*, every time a person comes in and out of the door, he encounters the unity of the Name of the Holy One, Blessed is He, and is reminded of His love. The person is aroused from his slumber, from his preoccupation with vain pursuits, and he realizes that nothing lasts forever and ever other than knowledge of the Creator of the Universe."

From which slumber must a person be awakened? The Rambam states clearly that it is his "preoccupation with vain pursuits." The only thing that has any lasting value is "knowledge of the Creator of the Universe."

Let us look back into *Hilchos Teshuvah*, and we will find almost identical language. "Wake up from your sleep, you who slumber, and examine your deeds. Remember your Creator, all those whose preoccupation with vain pursuits had led them to forget the truth, who devote all their years to foolish emptiness that is useless and ineffectual."

Wake up from your slumber! That, explains the Rambam, is the call of the *shofar*. Wake up!

Wake up? Who is sleeping?

Life itself, explains the Rambam, is one long slumber. We sleep through life. We spend our days and our years running after nothing, running after things that are meaningless, that have no lasting value. We pursue goals that are illusions, goals that we recognize in old age, or even sooner, as malignant mirages completely without substance.

That is the slumber of life. That is what our Sages wanted us to think about when we do *teshuvah*. Think about life. Think about what's meaningful in life. Consider that nothing in life matters but the spirit. Nothing in life delivers true satisfaction but spirituality.

Rav Shimon Schwab once made a beautiful observation about these words of the Rambam. Why is the *mezuzah* in particular meant to inspire us to think such deep thoughts about life?

Look at a *mezuzah*, said Rav Schwab. Picture in your mind a venerable building, perhaps hundreds of years old. Think about that *mezuzah* standing like a silent witness in the doorway. Think about what the *mezuzah* has seen over the long span of years, the generations that have come through those doors, the people that have passed in and out of those doors, the ideas that have crossed this threshold.

Think about all the ideologies, all the intellectual fads that were supposed to create utopias for humankind: The French Revolution, The Russian Revolution, Communism — bankrupt. Socialism — bankrupt. Humanism — bankrupt. The worship of science — bankrupt. All these have come and gone, but the *mezuzah* is still there. The *mezuzah*, and all it represents, is the only thing in this world that lasts. Only "knowledge of the Creator of the Universe" endures forever. In the final analysis, there is only one thing: the spirit. Spirituality gives us happiness. Spirituality gives us satisfaction.

I once read a story a woman wrote about her father. I don't know if the woman was Orthodox. But I do know that her story is so commonplace that each of us can readily think of a number of people about whom it could have been written. Perhaps that is what makes this story so powerful and moving.

The woman who wrote this story lived some distance from the home of her parents, and every year, she would return for Rosh Hashanah. Her father had suffered a stroke and was partially paralyzed. He would spend the entire Erev Rosh Hashanah — the entire day — getting ready for *shul*. Bathing, getting dressed, everything proceeded at a very slow pace. Finally, at the end of the day, he was ready for Rosh Hashanah.

Her father had built a small business which manufactured

and sold men's clothing, she tells us. He would leave the house at 6 in the morning and returned at 10 at night, even on Sundays. Over the years, the family's standard of living rose, but her father's work hours remained long and hard.

One Erev Rosh Hashanah, she asked her father to talk about his life.

"I had wanted to be rich," he said. "Not just for the money, but because being rich represented power, prestige. There was so much I could accomplish with money. I could give to charity, build synagogues, help the poor. I wanted to do those things. I wanted to make a name for myself, to be important." Doesn't this sound familiar?

Then the elderly man continued: "But it wasn't worth it. Even if I would have made it big, the sacrifices weren't worth it. I sacrificed my home life and my own life for the sake of making a reputation. I became a slave to my business. It was like the story of the pot of gold on the mountaintop. Climbers scrape and scratch their way up the mountain, salivating over that pot of gold. They are sure that if they don't reach the gold now they'll get there next year or the year after. Then they will be able to sit back and relax. But they never get there. Never."

Then the daughter asked if he was bitter about not getting to the top.

"No, I'm not bitter. I was disappointed for a long time. But now, it's not even that. It's more a matter of being sorry I didn't spend more time with my wife and children. I loved them so much."

Today, the daughter tells us that she can hardly remember the businessman he once was. She sees him rather as a gentle scholar whose greatest pleasure comes from studying and teaching Torah. More than 20 years ago, this man's goal changed, from wanting to accumulate wealth to wanting to accumulate knowledge. As his daughter notes, the second goal was by far more satisfying.

An old story. A common story.

All too many people look back from the vantage point of old age and ask themselves hard and painful questions. How much time and effort did I spend trying to find an elusive happiness? How much time and effort did I invest into becoming a partner of the firm? How much time and effort did I devote to making a six-figure salary? How much time and effort did I devote to starting my own practice? How much time and effort did I waste? How many futile sacrifices did I make?

One thing is for sure. In the end, we will all come to the same conclusion. It's not worth it, because it doesn't last. It never remains. The only thing that lasts, that remains, that makes a difference is spirituality.

When my father *alav hashalom* passed away a number of years ago, I grieved as does anyone who has the misfortune of losing a parent. After the *shivah* in Seattle, I said good-bye to my mother and returned to Baltimore. A few months later, my mother came for a visit. We had a nice time, and when she was ready to go home, I drove her to the airport.

It was an early morning flight. I remember it very vividly, and I remember taking leave of my mother on that cold morning just months after I had lost my father. It was terribly, terribly painful. It felt as if the whole tragedy had just happened again. I knew the scene to which my mother was returning. I knew she would face loneliness and sorrow all over again. And I felt terribly, terribly down about life. How futile it all was! Was is it all worth it?

I remember driving back on the Beltway and thinking that this is how we are all going to wind up, all of us. One day, we're either going to be dead, or we're going to be alone. How morose. How depressing.

I also remember my Shacharis that morning. I remember saying *Uva Letzion*, seeing its words light up in front of me as if for the very first time. How many thousands of times had I said these words before, yet never had they penetrated my heart as they did on that bleak winter morning. "*Hu yiftach libeinu besoraso* ... Let Him open our heart to His Torah. Let Him implant love for Him and awe of Him in our hearts so that we may fulfill His will, so that we may serve Him with sincere hearts, so that we should not toil in vain."

Why do we ask for this? So that we should not toil in vain. So that we should not pursue nothingness.

All of a sudden it just hit me like a ton of bricks. If you don't love Hashem, if you are not in awe of Hashem, if you don't have Torah, then you can't have a good life? It's all in vain? It's all emptiness? Isn't it possible to have happiness and satisfaction outside the realm of "loving Him and being in awe of Him"? And the answer is, no, it is not possible. Without spirituality, it's all "foolish emptiness." It is simply not worth it. The only thing that makes life worth living, the only thing that will save us from hopelessness and despair in old age is spirituality. If we can look on a life of spirituality, we will have the satisfaction of having lived well, of having done something meaningful and important. It's not the money. It's not the job. It's nothing but "knowledge of the Creator of the Universe." The rest is worthless.

My late father-in-law, Rav Yaakov Blumenkrantz, used to say that Moshe Rabbeinu was 10 cubits tall and the *Mishkan* he built was 10 cubits high. Clearly, a person is only as great as his accomplishments. If a person builds a personal *Mishkan* in this world, if he furnishes it with spirituality, with Torah, with *mitzvos*, with *chessed*, then he is indeed great. And the greater this personal *Mishkan*, the greater the person who built it.

That's what *teshuvah* is all about. Why should we do *teshuvah*? Why should we go through this process? Because it's good for us. Plain and simple. Because we'll feel better about it. We'll feel better about ourselves. We will be happier people. We will achieve that elusive goal called the pursuit of happiness. Nothing else will do it for us but spirituality, *ruchnius*.

Are we capable of doing it? We certainly are.

In Parshas *Ki Savo*, we read about *viduy maaser*. In the time of the *Beis Hamikdash,* when people brought *maaser sheni* to Jerusalem, they would declare, "I did not eat it during my bereavement. I obeyed every command You gave me." The commentators are puzzled. How does the word *viduy*, which means confession, apply to this declaration? *Viduy* is *chatasi, avisi, pashati,* I transgressed, I sinned, I bear guilt. But how does this claim of following all the rules qualify as a *Viduy*?

Rav Yoshe Ber Soloveitchik explains that there are two aspects to *Viduy* which make it effective. One aspect involves the ability of a person to face up to his sins, to acknowledge them and accept responsibility for them. That is very important. "I have transgressed. I have sinned. I bear guilt." But there is a second aspect which is also critical. A person must believe that he is capable of improvement, of reaching higher spiritual levels. He has to aspire to spiritual growth. "I obeyed every command You gave me." If a person does not believe he is capable of growth, if he does not aspire to higher spiritual levels, then a mere confession of sins is not a viable *Viduy*. What's the point of getting down on yourself if you can't lift yourself up?

The *Yamim Nora'im* season is the time when we look back at the year that has gone by. We think about it. We think about the coming year. And what do we say? It hasn't been the year that we expected it to be. We had such grand plans last Rosh Hashanah. Now it hasn't turned out like we wanted.

The Torah tells us (*Devarim* 11:12) that Hashem watches "*mereishis hashanah ve'ad acharis shanah,* from the beginning of the year until year's end." Our Sages understand this as a reference to Rosh Hashanah.

The Satmar Rav points out a grammatical anomaly in this phrase. The first mention of the year features a definite article, *mereishis hashanah,* from the beginning of *the* year, but the second mention has no article at all, *acharis shanah,* year's end.

I believe we can all relate to the Satmar Rav's answer, because we recognize it from experience. This is the way of life. The year always starts out with a bang. This is going to be *the* year. This is going to be the year we are going to learn more Torah. This is going to be the year we give more *tzedakah*. This is going to be the year we stop speaking *lashon hara*. This year we will be more considerate of our children, our spouses, our family and friends.

But what happens at the end of the year? We find ourselves at year's end — not *the* year, just a year. Ordinary, a little disappointing. A year like any other year, undeserving of definite articles.

In the Mussaf *Kedushah* according to Nusach Sefard, we find the words "*hein ga'alti es'chem acharis kereishis,*" when *Mashiach* comes the end will be like the beginning. When *Mashiach* comes, explains the Satmar Rav, our years will end with the same high ideals and enthusiasm as they began. We will look back and not be disappointed.

But until then, what can we do? How do we keep up the momentum with which the year begins? The answer is careful and realistic planning.

Make a written plan. Take off a few hours and come home early from work. Help in the house. Learn with the children. Say *Tehillim.* And then, once you are in the proper frame of mind, take out a sheet of paper and write down what you are going to do in the new year.

Start with something small, but whatever it is, make sure you write it down. Make sure you keep that paper handy, and refer back to it often. Little by little, you will see your life improve. You will see your life illuminated by the infusion of spirituality.

And you will discover that all the happiness you have been pursuing so diligently has been well within your grasp from the very beginning.

CONTEMPORARY ISSUES

Jews on the Career Track

A N ATTORNEY IN BALTIMORE, MARYLAND, WHO IS A friend of mine, was involved in a very large real estate deal. The other party was represented by the law firm of Baker and Mackenzie in New York City. For those of you who are unfamiliar with the legal world, let me tell you that Baker and Mackenzie happens to be the largest law firm in the world.

This was a very high-powered and complex deal, and the attorney from Baker and Mackenzie had to come down quite often to Baltimore to meet with my friend, the attorney for the other party. Naturally, they did lunch and had dinner. Since my friend is an Orthodox Jew, and since Baltimore does not have an overabundance of elegant kosher eateries, they were basically limited to two restaurants.

The attorney from Baker and Mackenzie was not Jewish. He knew very little about Jews, and practically nothing about Orthodox Jews. He knew absolutely nothing about kosher, but he respected my friend's customs and had no problem limiting his meals to these two restaurants. In fact, he was quite fascinated by the lifestyle of an Orthodox Jew.

As the negotiations proceeded, the scene eventually shifted from Baltimore to New York, and my friend was invited to visit the New York offices of Baker and Mackenzie.

"When you get up here," the non-Jewish attorney told him, "lunch will be my treat. Unfortunately, we won't have the time to go out to a restaurant, but I'll order a nice spread sent up to one of our conference rooms with a view of the skyline. What would you like?"

"Whatever you like," my friend replied. "By the way, don't forget that I only eat kosher."

"How could I forget?" said the man from Baker and Mackenzie. "Not only do I remember you need kosher, I also remember that you have specific preferences with regard to the rabbinical supervision. Name a restaurant anywhere in the city that you consider reliable, and I'll order their best. How about Lou G. Segal? It's on Thirty-eighth Street, right off Seventh Avenue. Is that okay?"

"I see you've done your homework," my friend replied. "Lou G. Segal is just fine."

The next morning, the attorney called Lou G. Segal, determined to order something special and very expensive for lunch. He asked for a menu to be faxed to his office.

"Which menu would you like, sir?" he was asked.

The attorney was puzzled. "The kosher menu?" he ventured.

"Sir, we only serve kosher. Next week is Passover, and we have a special Passover menu. Would you like our regular menu or our special Passover menu?"

Aha! thought the attorney. A special Passover menu. That sounds just right. "I'll take the special menu, of course," he said.

Minutes later, he was sitting at his desk, poring over the Passover menu. Nothing on it made any sense. When in doubt, he decided, order the most expensive item — which is exactly what he did.

At lunchtime, he invited the attorney from Baltimore into the conference room with the view. Sure enough, the lunch he ordered from Lou G. Segal was waiting for them on the table. It was in an enormous, plastic-covered box. They both stared at it.

"This is your lunch?" asked my friend.

The other attorney shrugged. "Let's open it and see what it is."

They opened the package gingerly, and what was in it?

A seder plate! A large seder plate, complete with *marror*, *charoses*, a hard-boiled egg, a broiled shank bone and *shemurah matzah*.

"You have interesting tastes," said the attorney from Baltimore. "This is very nice, but I would have been satisfied with corned beef on rye."

When I heard this story, I laughed until my sides hurt, but there is also a rather dismal side to this bizarre scenario. The professional world in which my attorney friend works belongs to Baker and Mackenzie, and as nice as they are to him, he is nonetheless an alien presence. For myself, I am forever grateful to Hashem for the *zchus* of living in a safe, enclosed world which basically encompasses my *beis midrash*, my townhouse and the 400 yards in between. But those of you who perform in the professional arena are spending a substantial part of your time in what is literally foreign territory.

You are entering an environment that doesn't even begin to understand what you are all about. In fact, you really should carry a passport with you every single morning when you go to work. Why? Because you are going from your strong Jewish enclaves, wherever they may be, into a foreign country, a country that does not understand about *kashrus*, that doesn't understand about Shabbos, that doesn't understand about Pesach.

Even more fundamentally, you are entering a world that has an entirely different value system from that of the Orthodox Jew, a value system that is entirely inimical to Torah values. Let me explain.

Your non-Jewish counterparts out there in corporate America or business America or professional America always define their being by how they make a living. That is who they are. They are their professions. Therefore, according to their mindset, a person must have a career of distinction in order to be a person of distinction. And nothing less.

You always hear about the different "isms" that are the scourge of the Jewish people — humanism, socialism and so forth. Well, let me present to you another insidious "ism" which causes tremendous damage to our people — careerism. In fact, in today's world, which is so bereft of idealism and ideology, careerism looms as the most menacing "ism" of all.

In contemporary society, a person is nothing unless he succeeds in his profession. Otherwise, he is a failure. To be a person of distinction, one must have a career of distinction. That's the equation. A person of distinction equals a career of distinction. That's what America is all about.

What happens when two people are thrown together on a train or a plane? They usually strike up a conversation. Usually within the first three minutes of the conversation, one of them will ask, "So what do you do?"

"What do you do?" What does he mean by that? Is he talking about family? No. Is he talking about politics? No. Is he talking about religion? Certainly not. So what is he talking about? He is talking about professions. Careers. What do you do for a living? What do you do professionally?

Why is this question so urgent, so critical, that it comes up so quickly? Very simple. Because in contemporary American society the only way you measure, evaluate and know people is by what they do professionally. If you want to know some-one, to understand him, find out what he does for a living.

Think about it. Think about how children are conditioned to this mindset from early childhood. We ask a little boy or a little girl, "What do you want to be when you grow up?" And they are expected to answer, "I want to be a doctor, a lawyer, an accountant, a dentist, a businessperson." But that is not really the appropriate answer. The question was, What do you want to *be*? The answer, however, only addresses what they want to *do*. Unfortunately, in contemporary society, those are one and the same thing. You are what you do. Who are you? I'm a doctor. I'm a lawyer. That's who I am. That's what defines me. And unless I achieve success at my pro-fession, I am a failure.

This is not a Torah value. It is the opposite of what a Jew should be.

The Brisker Rav once asked a visitor, "*Vas zent ihr?* What are you?"

"I am a businessman," the visitor replied.

The Brisker Rav shook his head. "*Vas zent ihr?*" he asked again.

"I am a businessman," the visitor repeated.

"*Aber vas zent ihr?*" the Brisker Rav persisted. "But what are you?"

Clearly there was a communication problem. Perhaps, the man thought, the Brisker Rav might be a little hard of hearing. So he repeated his answer once again, this time raising his voice a few decibels.

"You don't have to yell," the Brisker Rav told him. "I heard you perfectly well the first time. But you don't seem to understand the question. A Jew is not defined by what he does for a living. Let me tell you about Yonah Hanavi on the boat. As the storm was raging, the sailors asked him, '*Ma melachtecha?* What do you do?' So what did Yonah reply? Did he tell them he was a prophet? Not at all. He said, '*Ivri anochi, v'es Hashem Elokei hashamayim ani yarei.* I am a

Jew, and I fear the Lord of the Heavens.' There's only one answer to the question *vos tust du*, what do you do. It is *Ivri anochi*. I'm a Jew. *V'es elokei hashamayim ani yarei*. And I fear the Lord of the Heavens. Do you understand?"

The visitor nodded, obviously chastened.

"Business is not what you are," the Brisker Rav told him. "Business is what the *Ribono Shel Olam* gives you. But what are you? The only answer is, *Ivri anochi*, I'm a devout Jew."

That answer, that concept, that what defines us as being devout Jews is so alien to the secular world. They cannot conceive that a person would be defined by his relationship with the Almighty. But according to the Torah, that is what it's all about. There's nothing else that should matter. *Ivri Anochi*. I am a devout Jew.

I have a life-long friend, someone with whom I went to kindergarten in Seattle, Washington. He is an exceptional person, brilliant, talented, a *baal midos* of the first order. He still lives in Seattle and works as a systems analyst for Boeing, the huge aircraft manufacturer.

Some time ago, we were discussing his job, and he told me he had made an important career decision. Over the years, he had risen in the company in accordance with his considerable abilities, and by this time he had reached a certain level at which he is reasonably secure financially. He has now decided that this is as far as it goes. He's not interested in any further advancement. He wants to be able to come to work at 8:30 in the morning and leave at 4:30 in the afternoon.

He doesn't want subordinates answering to him. He doesn't want to travel on business. He doesn't want to stay late for managerial conferences. He wants to come home, learn with his children, learn for himself, even if it means earning less money. It was his life, and this was how he wanted to live it.

When he told his superiors at Boeing about his decision, they looked at him as if he had just landed from Mars. Had he taken leave of his senses? Here was a talented guy, brilliant in fact. He had all the tools. He could rise high in the corporate hierarchy. He could make a lot of money. He could earn a fancy title and get a plush office. How could he turn all this down? And if he didn't care about these things, what was he doing there in the first place?

The answer, which they couldn't fathom, is that he did not buy into the corporate culture. What defined him? *Ivri anochi.* As long as he could support his family on a decent standard, he didn't need the rest of the benefits and privileges that the corporate world has to offer.

I once met a fellow who had heard me speak to a gathering about the concept of *Ivri anochi.* He told me that he works for Chase Manhattan Bank, and for a variety of reasons, he can't wear his *yarmulke* at work.

"I sit there in my office bareheaded," he said, "but I want to feel Jewish. So I went ahead and photocopied that *passuk* you mentioned. *Ivri anochi, v'es Hashem elokei hashamayim ani yarei.* I put the paper under the glass on my desk, because that's what I want to know every day of my working life. And if I cannot wear the *yarmulke* that's supposed to remind me of that, I want to be able to stare at that *passuk.*"

This tension between being a good Torah Jew and maintaining a professional life, of balancing the two worlds, inspired a former *talmid* to write to Rav Yitzchak Hutner .

"I feel as if I am leading a double life," he wrote. "What should I do?"

Rav Hutner replied with his inimitable insight and clarity. "It is apparent from your question," he wrote, "that you equate a secular career with a double life. I would never approve of a *talmid* of mine living a double life. But let me present to you the following analogy. If a person rents a house to use as his permanent residence and then he goes ahead and rents a room elsewhere in the same town, he is definitely living a double life. He has one house where he lives and another place that he visits. That's a double life. But should he rent a house that has more than one room, would that be living a double life? No, that is not a double life, it is a broad life. You can be a good Torah Jew and still have a secular career without leading a double life. You can have a house with many rooms."

And then Rav Hutner writes, "I remember visiting the famous Dr. Wallach's hospital in Jerusalem. I saw a patient being wheeled into surgery, and I heard Dr. Wallach ask him, 'What's your mother's name?' He then went off to say some *Tehillim* for this man before operating on him. Tell me, was Dr. Wallach leading a double life? Or was he fusing the life of the doctor with the life of the Jew? That's not a double life. I told this story to one of the *gedolim* of Jerusalem, and he expressed his envy of people like Dr. Wallach who can fuse the two sides of their lives together."

Is there a bigger instrument of *kiddush shem Shamayim* than a doctor who says *Tehillim* for his patient? This man knows that the Healer controls all health, that he is but the Almighty's humble instrument. This man is not a doctor on the one hand and a Jew on the other. He has achieved an exalted fusion of his doctoring and his Jewishness. This is what a secular career can provide a person.

Rav Hutner concludes with a classic play on words. "My dear and precious *talmid*, do not consider yourself as a person living two lives. You have to be a *maarich be'echad*." According to the Gemara in *Berachos*, whoever stretches out the saying of the word *echad* during *Krias Shema* is given long life. Extend your *echad*, Rav Hutner was telling his *talmid*. Expand the one figurative house in which you live to encompass all the facets of your complex life in a single fused and exalted whole. That is not a double life but a life that is exquisitely full.

That is how we have to view ourselves in the professional world. That is how a person should view a secular career. That's the paradigm. Go ahead and have the two-room house. There is no contradiction, no paradox, as long as both rooms are under one roof.

But I would like to extend Rav Hutner's analogy just a bit. A person can have a house with many rooms but treat them differently. One room he decorates lavishly, with expensive furniture, carpets, window treatments and so forth. The other room he leaves bare — no carpeting, no wallpaper, no fixtures, nothing but bare walls. Then he spends practically all his time in the decorated room, but hardly any time in the bare room. Is that living a broad life or a double life?

This then is the tremendous *nisayon* of the Jew in the professional world. Is he spending all his time in one of the rooms or is he giving equal time and effort to both rooms?

If you are a successful professional, whether a good lawyer, a good accountant, a good dentist, a good businessman or a good any other, you undoubtedly invest a lot of sweat and toil in your profession. You give it everything you've got, and you get a real charge out of it. It is surely exhilarating to come up with a clever strategy to save your client a bundle of money, to structure the deal, to see the diagnosis, to do the procedure with precision. It is only natural that you should find that thrilling.

But what about the *Ivri anochi?* Does it get at least an equal investment of time, energy and effort? Far be it from me to tell anyone not to enjoy his job, not to be a good lawyer, not to be a good professional. It would be wrong to do such a thing. A person has to give his all to everything important that he does. But that goes a thousandfold for his religious life, for his Jewishness, for his relationship with the Creator of the Universe. It is not enough to go through the motions. Something has to make your life tick, other than the job.

"And you shall safeguard the statutes and laws that a person must do so that he may live by them." (*Vayikra* 18:5) The exact words are *vechai bahem*, so that he may live by them. The Chiddushei HaRim understands these words to mean that a person has to draw his *chiyus*, his vitality, from the performance of the *mitzvos*. He can't just fulfill his obligations perfunctorily. They have to become his very breath of life.

People today are learning *Daf Yomi*. That's a wonderful thing, a complete *daf* every day. But what has the *Daf Yomi* become? Has it become merely like saying *Tehillim* or *Ashrei*? Do we *daven* the *Daf Yomi*? Do people who have the ability to learn more content themselves with *Daf Yomi*, thinking that they've fulfilled their daily Torah study obligations and can now spend some time on other pursuits? Does learning *Daf Yomi* get them off the hook, so to speak?

People have to challenge themselves. For some, learning *Daf Yomi* even on a superficial level is without doubt a tremendous achievement. For others, simply learning a little *Mishnayos* is a daunting challenge. But if you're beyond that, then *Daf Yomi* does not get you off the hook. You have to plunge into the depths of the *Yam HaTalmud* with all your strength and skills. You have to live in it — and live from it.

It is not enough to get your thrills, your excitement, your exhilaration from your career. You have to get at least as much from the *Ivri anochi*. Because if you don't, that Jewish room in your house will remain bare and unfurnished.

How do we assure that we have that Jewish spark in our lives? We have to set goals for ourselves, to develop absorbing projects, whether in learning or *chessed* or any other *dvar ruchnius*. Even rabbis know that they must become involved in important projects if they don't want to fall into a rut in their Jewishness. If it's not learning, then it can be creating a *bikur cholim* or *hachnassas orchim* organization, raising money for *hachnassas kallah*, or even getting involved in *shidduchim*.

Yes, *shidduchim*. There is such a dire need for people to get involved in *shidduchim*, not for the money but for the *mitzvah*. If you want *Olam Haba*, this is a guaranteed route. Someone once pointed out to me at an Agudah convention that if every person in attendance would undertake to make five *shidduchim* in their lifetimes, just five *shidduchim*, it would change the face of *Klal Yisrael*.

Some people have undertaken to put meticulous observance of the laws against speaking *lashon hara* back on the map, and on the radar screen, by organizing and promoting *Machsom Lefi*. That's a project that can become a *vechai bahem*, that can provide your vitality, your breath of life from your Jewishness.

The Torah tells us, "And he loved Rachel more than Leah … and Hashem saw that Leah was hated" (*Bereishis* 29:30-31). Can it be that the great and holy Jacob hated his wife Leah? Heaven forbid, writes Rav Shimon Schwab. *Ve'ahavta le'rei'acha kamocha!* Love your neighbor as yourself. If the Torah tells us to love our neighbors, we certainly have to love our wives at least as much. There is, therefore, absolutely no doubt that Jacob loved Leah.

What then does the Torah mean by telling us that "Leah was hated"?

Here Rav Schwab makes a very insightful observation. In any love relationship, he writes, the person loved must be paramount to all others. Anything less is tantamount to hate. If a person has two wives and loves one more than the other, the wife less loved is by definition the hated one. A wife has to be the focus of her husband's love, the object of his absolute and undivided devotion. Rachel enjoyed that position. Leah did not. Therefore, Hashem considered her to be hated.

The same applies to the *Ivri anochi*. The Torah tells us to love Hashem, to make Him the focus of our lives. Hashem cannot play second fiddle, not to the business, not to the firm, not to anything else whatsoever.

The best way to make sure that Hashem is not relegated to second fiddle status to our careers is to channel those self-same careers into His service, just as Dr. Wallach in Jerusalem used his medical practice to serve Hashem.

Let me share with you a personal incident. Some time ago, my mother had to undergo emergency bypass surgery in Seattle. It was a very tumultuous 72 hours from the time my mother was first taken to the hospital until she finally went into surgery. At the first hint of trouble, I flew out to

Seattle, but I didn't know where to begin. It was a long way from my childhood days there. Things had changed. I didn't know the doctors. I didn't know the hospitals. I felt lost.

Fortunately, I remembered a cardiologist who had moved from Baltimore to Seattle. I decided to call him up. "David, what do these things mean?" I asked him. "What's the prognosis? What should I do?"

For those next three days and beyond, this doctor was my own Dr. Wallach, literally and figuratively holding my hand.

When they decided my mother had to have surgery and transferred her to the University of Washington Medical Center, I was completely out of my depth.

"Who's the doctor?" I asked the nurse.

"You'll meet him in a minute," she replied.

A few minutes later, the doctor came by. I looked at his white gown. I looked at his face. "I'm Dr. Salaam Aziz," he said. "I will be upstairs if you need me."

Salaam Aziz? Not a typical name among the doctors I know.

"So what have you decided?" the hospital people wanted to know. "Are you or are you not going to do the surgery?"

In desperation, I called David. "You're on the staff here, David," I said. "Have you ever heard of this guy?"

"No, I can't say that I have," he replied, "but this is a big hospital. Find out whether he's an attending physician. If he's an attending physician on the staff of the University of Washington Medical Center, you know you're not going to be too far off the mark."

I hung up and went back to find Dr. Aziz. Fortunately, he was still there.

"Dr. Aziz," I said, "are you an attending physician?"

"Yes, I am," he said with a twinkle in his eye.

"Then let's go ahead with the surgery."

As it turned out Dr. Aziz, who is from India, is a wonderfully skilled and caring surgeon. David was able, using his expertise, his career, to be a Jew first and a doctor second.

When my mother went into surgery at 3 o'clock in the afternoon, I settled in for the eight-hour wait. There I was all by myself in a hospital waiting room in Seattle. My wife was in Baltimore. My brother was traveling in New Zealand. My sister was in Chicago. My mother was in surgery. I was all alone.

But not quite. At 5 o'clock in the afternoon, David showed up.

"Hi," he said. "Do you have any room for me here? I'm staying with you."

"David, go home," I said. "I appreciate your offer, but it's really not necessary. You've been at work the whole day, and your family needs you. Go home. I'll be just fine."

"Nothing doing. I'm staying with you."

And that was that. For the next few hours, he sat by my side giving me moral support and just plain keeping me company. I can recall few times in my life when I was so thankful to see a familiar face. It was an act of true *chessed*, and I will always be grateful.

Here is a man who was *maarich be'echad*, who was able to fuse his career with his Jewishness. Here is a person who was able to sanctify the *gashmius*, to elevate the secular and make it holy. There are few things dearer to Hashem than that.

When Moshe Rabbeinu was building the *Mishkan*, the women wanted to donate the mirrors they had used for beautifying themselves for their husbands. Moshe Rabbeinu was reluctant to take these mirrors. He didn't think they were appropriate for the sanctified utensils of the *Mishkan*.

But Hashem told Moshe Rabbeinu to use the mirrors. Why? Because there had been a time when the Jewish men enslaved in Egypt had refused to bring children into this world. It was bad enough that they themselves had to suffer, but why bring innocent new life into this blighted bondage? But the women said no, life must go on. They beautified themselves in front of those mirrors and went out to their husbands in the fields, and so they bore young Jewish children. "These mirrors," said Hashem, "are more precious to me than all the rest."

These women had taken something profane, something secular, something material, and they had elevated it into *ruchnius*. What could be more holy?

If a person can take his career, his profession and elevate it into *ruchnius,* this is indeed precious to Hashem.

Is it easy?

No, it is not.

Is it fraught with danger?

Yes, it is.

Can it be done?

Most definitely.

A friend of mine from my *yeshivah* days was considering becoming a doctor, and he asked the Ponevezher Rav for his advice.

"Tell me," said the Ponevezher Rav, "have you heard the news about the man who walked across Niagara Falls on a tightrope?"

"Yes, I did," my friend replied.

"Well if he would have come beforehand to ask my advice, I would have said he was crazy. But now that he's successfully done it, he is an international hero. What should I tell you? Is the path to becoming a doctor fraught with danger? Without doubt. But if a person is successful, he can use it to make a *kiddush Hashem*."

"So what should I do?" asked my friend.

"You have to arrange a safety net," said the Ponevezher Rav, "before you walk across the falls on a tightrope."

My friend took the Ponevezher Rav's advice. Today, he is an outstanding physician and an even more outstanding Jew.

Every one of us who steps into the secular world, who ventures into the professional arena, must be fully aware that he or she is walking across a roaring falls on a tightrope. And he has to make sure that there are safety nets to catch him if he stumbles.

What are those safety nets? Our homes; our *yeshivos*; our *rabbanim*; our spouses, who can tell their mates when they're veering from the path; the time we set aside for learning Torah and doing *mitzvos*. All of these are our safety nets, without which going out into the world would be like crossing Niagara Falls on a tightrope, foolhardy and dangerous.

That has to be our goal — to stay close to our safety nets as we bring honor and glory to His great and holy Name.

Quality Adjusted Life Years

FIRST IMPRESSIONS CAN BE MISLEADING. MANY ISSUES may seem perfectly benign at first glance, posing no threat to our Torah way of life, but upon further reflection, they are revealed as fundamentally incompatible with the Torah view. And this creates a great problem for us, because by the time we identify a concept as alien to Judaism, it may already have insinuated itself into our consciousness, causing damage that may be difficult to repair.

Rashi in *Parashas Vayechi* observes that this *parashah* is a *setumah*, that there is no space separating it from the previous *parashah*. Why? It is meant to symbolize, Rashi tells us, that when Yaakov passed away "*nistemu eineihem veliban shel Yisrael mitzoras hashibud*," the eyes and hearts of the Jewish people were beclouded by the difficulty of their oppression.

The commentators immediately ask: What oppression? We all know that the oppression of the Jewish people did not begin until all of Yaakov's sons passed away many years later.

The Sfas Emes explains that, although the actual physical bondage did not begin until many years later, a profound change in the Jewish people occurred when Yaakov passed away, a change that affected their eyes and their hearts. What does this mean? It means that the sensitivity of their Jewish eyes and their Jewish hearts was diminished. A Jewish person views the world through Jewish eyes, with a particular *Weltanschauung* formed by Torah values and ideals. He reacts to the world with a Jewish heart, with specifically Jewish feelings and attitudes. But when Yaakov passed away, this special sensitivity was blunted, clouded, dulled. The absolute Jewishness of their perspective was compromised.

If that's what our Sages tell us about the exalted children and grandchildren of Yaakov Avinu, what can we say about our own humble generation?

In the modern world, we suffer terribly from this blunted perspective. It is hard for us to distinguish between those ideas that are part of long-standing Jewish tradition and those ideas that are of recent vintage and foreign to the Torah.

Let me give you an example. It involves a recent news item from California, the greenhouse of innovative American thought. It seems that the state has established a new commission to study self-esteem.

Self-esteem. What an intriguing and beguiling concept. The media has labeled self-esteem as the elixir of the Nineties, the panacea for all ills, from poor grades to bad management. Who can be against self-esteem? What can be objectionable about the State of California seeking to promote self-esteem among its citizens?

Is there anything not Jewish about self-esteem?

On the contrary, self-esteem is a very Jewish concept.

Rabbeinu Yonah writes in his introduction to *Shaar Avodah*, "The gateway to becoming a true servant of Hashem is to know one's own worth." There you have it. Self-esteem! A person has to know who he is.

But upon further reflection, we discover a wide and gaping chasm between the Torah view of self-esteem and the contemporary version. Self-esteem derives from an appreciation of one's own worthiness, but how is that worthiness measured? In modern society, which is so productivity oriented, worthiness is determined by one thing: the capacity to perform and to produce. A person who is no longer able to produce is no longer considered worthy. But according to the Torah view, worthiness is not determined by what you do but by who you are.

The Dubno Maggid makes this point very clearly with regard to the relationship of Yitzchak and Rivkah to their children. The Torah tells us (*Bereishis* 25:28): "And Yitzchak loved Eisav because he ate his trapped game, but Rivkah loves Yaakov." The commentators are puzzled. Why is the relationship between Yitzchak and Eisav expressed in the past tense, "and Yitzchak loved Eisav," while the relationship between Rivkah and Yaakov is expressed in the present tense, "and Rivkah loves Yaakov"?

With someone like an Eisav, the Dubno Maggid explains, his only worthiness derived from the trapped game he delivered rather than his personal qualities. And if a person's worth is determined by what he does, it is always in the past tense, because what you've done is always in the past. As they say in America, "What have you done for me lately?" That's the measuring rod. What have you done? What have you accomplished? On the other hand, "Rivkah loves Yaakov" because of who he is, and therefore, that love remains constant, always in the present tense.

Ask a kid in America, "What do you want to be when you grow up?" Do you know what he will invariably answer? That he wants to be a doctor, a lawyer, a captain of industry, a rabbi, a teacher and so on. But all these do not answer the question. You asked him what he wants to be, but he tells you what he wants to do. Do you know why? Because that's America. Being is doing. Your whole essence of a person, his entire sense of self is determined by what he does. That's why in America, when two strangers strike up a conversation, one of the first questions will be, "So what do you do for a living?" I read that someone was so annoyed by this question that he would respond, "I'm an undercover agent for the IRS." End of conversation.

But that is the way things are. This is the order of the questions. What's your name? What do you do? And the second question is more fundamental than the first. Because in America, what you do defines who you are.

But do these different conceptual approaches to personal worthiness affect us in a practical way?

They most certainly do. If worthiness is productivity, then modern society must rethink what makes life itself important. And the inevitable conclusion is that what makes life important is its active participation in society. This, in turn, spawns a new term called quality of life. What does this mean? It means that life is only valuable when it has a certain measurable quality, a very disturbing thought.

In the lexicon of the Torah, however, there is no such word, no such terminology. The Torah does not speak of the quality of life but the sanctity of life, because by its eternal standards, all human life has value. Every single human life is a spark of the Divine.

The Torah demands that we desecrate the Shabbos to rescue even the most tenuous of lives, but that flies in the face of the modern attitude towards life. In modern society, where worthiness depends on productivity, the unborn, the infirm, the terminally ill are all viewed as intolerable and very expendable burdens that interfere with our quality of life.

That explains why American society declares, in diverse and subtle ways, that certain lives are just not worth living.

That may explain why 23 million unborn infants have been aborted in America since 1973.

That explains why Richard Lamm, the former governor of Colorado, can declare explicitly what others imply with subtlety, "The elderly have a duty to die and get out of the way."

Self-esteem based on productivity. Quality of life. Get out of the way and die. That's the modern perspective.

Modern attitudes toward life have so indoctrinated our society with the concept of the quality of life that a life of suffering is automatically considered meaningless and worthless. A dying patient in a hospital, helpless and suffering, how can this life possibly have meaning? And if it doesn't, why bother to preserve it?

According to our eternal Torah, however, life always has intrinsic value. Every soul was sent down to this world for a specific amount of time. That is its purpose. And therefore, every additional moment that the soul spends in this world is infinitely precious.

In one of his books, Rabbi Abraham J. Twerski, M.D. describes how he visited a young woman, the mother of two little children, who suffered from multiple sclerosis. She was deteriorating, blind and helpless, a total burden to her family, and not surprisingly, she was deeply depressed.

What could you say to such a woman? Dr. Twerski related to her the following Gemara (*Sanhedrin* 101a):

The rabbis taught: When Rabbi Eliezer fell ill, four sages came to visit him, Rabbi Tarfon, Rabbi Yehoshua, Rabbi Elazar ben Azariah and Rabbi Akiva.

Rabbi Tarfon spoke up and said: "You are more precious to the Jewish people than the raindrops, because raindrops only bring benefit in this world while you bring benefit in this world and the next."

Rabbi Yehoshua spoke up and said: "You are more precious to the Jewish people than the sun, because the sun only brings benefit in this world while you bring benefit in this world and the next."

Rabbi Elazar ben Azariah spoke up and said: "You are more precious to the Jewish people than parents, because parents only bring benefit in this world while you bring benefit in this world and the next."

Rabbi Akiva spoke up and said: "Suffering is precious."

[Rabbi Eliezer] said to them: "Prop me up so that I can hear the words of my disciple Akiva."

The question immediately arises: Why did Rabbi Akiva's words bring greater consolation to Rabbi Eliezer than the words of the other sages?

Let us think about Rabbi Eliezer's situation. He is lying on his deathbed, completely helpless. He knows that his days of teaching Torah are over, that he will never again open the eyes of a new *talmid* to the wonders of the Torah. He knows that it is all over. So what do the other sages say to him? That he is as precious as raindrops, the sun, parents? But that is all in the past. Never again will he bring anyone benefit in this world or in the next. And so, there is little consolation in these words.

But Rabbi Akiva tells him something else entirely. Rabbi Akiva tells him that there is still something great he can do right now, even as he lies stretched out on his deathbed. What is that? He can accept the suffering he has been allotted with faith and love, and therefore, even in his diminished state, his life still has a purpose.

Indeed, that is all the Almighty ever asks of a person. That is all He ever expects of us. A person does not have to make a so-called "productive" contribution to society. All he needs to do is fulfill to the best of his ability his role as a servant of the Almighty. And if that entails merely lying in a bed and suffering, then that is more than sufficient.

This is what Dr. Twerski told the young mother dying of multiple sclerosis. More than anything else he could have said, these words brought her consolation and peace.

In a similar vein, I would like to relate an amazing story that happened to a *talmid* of mine. This young man had once attended Columbia University, and from time to time, he would return to participate in outreach programs on the campus. Last year, he went back to Columbia University for a Shabbaton.

On Friday night, he was sitting at the table with some of the best and brightest students of Columbia University. There were also a number of mentally retarded children in attendance, brought there by an organization called Yachad, an organization for the developmentally disabled.

"Every Jew has a role in life," the young man was telling his rapt audience. "Just as no two letters in the Torah may touch each other, no Jew can infringe on the purpose and mission of another Jew. Everyone has his role."

Just then a 17 year-old Yachad boy raised his hand. "I have a question," he said. "What is my role? I'm mentally disabled. I can't do anything. So what is my role in life?"

Then the boy started to cry. Within moments, tears were streaming down the faces of most of the Columbia college boys as well.

This very powerful question faced the young man. What is my role?

Thinking quickly, he came up with an excellent answer. "You want to know what your role is?" he said. "I'll tell you. You asked a question. You made people think. You made people cry. You touched people. That's your role. You asked an important question."

A week later, just one week later, the young man received a telephone call. The 17 year-old boy from Yachad had gotten up one morning and told his mother he wasn't feeling well. A few hours later, he died.

The young man went to pay a *shivah* call, wondering what he could say to the parents. But before he had a chance to say anything, his father said, "You know, my son fulfilled his role. He asked his question. Maybe that was why he was sent down to this world."

This is a true story.

So this is the Torah perspective on life. A person's life is precious even if he is not being "productive." Maybe all he has to do is ask a question. Maybe all he has to do is lie on his bed and suffer in silence. There may not be much quality of life as we understand it, but there is plenty of sanctity of life.

But let us take a look at where the contemporary obsession with quality of life is leading society. Let us take the issue of health care reform. If universal health care is going to happen, costs will have to be controlled. In other words, using the term which is on everyone's mind but no one wants to utter, there will be rationing. Health care reform equals health care rationing.

And where do you think those cuts are going to be? The first people who will be denied health care are those whose quality of life is deemed inferior. According to studies, 40 percent of a person's health care costs are incurred during the last few months of his life. Think about it. 40 percent of a lifetime's worth of health care expenses is incurred in the last few months. So won't this be the perfect place to make some deep cuts?

There are professional people today whose job it is to make these assessments. They categorize treatment costs in terms of QALYs. Quality adjusted life years. This is how they try to make a determination on these cost issues. Is it cost-effective to spend $40,000 on a cardiac defibrillator for an old person with bad lungs and bad kidneys? How many QALYs (quality adjusted life years) can he have? These are the questions that will be considered by the bureaucrat in Washington before he makes his life-and-death decision.

But let us take a look at what the Meiri says in *Yoma* 83a. The Mishnah tells us a pile of bricks may be moved on Shabbos if there is a possibility of rescuing a person trapped underneath. But what if after they start to excavate they discover that the person trapped underneath is on the verge of death, that he cannot live for even another hour?

Nonetheless, rules the Meiri, the excavation must go forward to preserve the last few minutes of the trapped person's life. Why? Because maybe in those few minutes he "may repent and confess his sins." Maybe he will have a *hirhur teshuvah*. This little but transcendent moment makes life worthwhile and necessitates the desecration of the Shabbos to preserve it.

But how would the bureaucrat in Washington see it? How does modern society look at it? When they see a comatose person, do you think they would make an effort to give him a few lucid moments so that he might still have a *hirhur teshuvah*? Not a chance. He has no QALYs left. There is no quality of life.

There are, of course, many *halachic* issues that must be addressed by a qualified *posek* when a patient is in extremis, and it is not my intention to imply that there is no limit to the heroic measures that must be taken to preserve that final moment of life. But the well-meaning doctor may come and say to the family, "I'm sorry, but there's no quality of life." Remember, this doctor doesn't know about *hirhurei teshuvah*. He doesn't know about Divine sparks and the time allotted to a *neshamah* in this world.

Rabbi J. D. Bleich writes about his maternal grandmother who suffered kidney failure and was comatose for 36 hours. He came into the hospital, looked at the chart and saw that there was nothing being done for his grandmother.

He called the doctor to complain. "Why aren't you doing anything for her?"

"Listen," said the doctor, "she's an old lady. Let her go in peace and dignity."

Rabbi Bleich considered the doctor's words. Intellectually, he knew what his decision had to be, but emotionally, it was difficult.

"Treat her," he said. "Try to keep her alive as long as you can."

And so they started treating her.

On Shabbos, Rabbi Bleich came into the hospital room. "Good Shabbos," he said to his grandmother.

Then this old woman, who had been comatose for 36 hours, opened half an eye and responded, "Good Shabbos."

A few hours later, she passed away.

Do you realize what just happened here? Rabbi Akiva Eiger writes in his commentary to the *Shulchan Aruch* that when a person says "Good Shabbos" he fulfills a *mitzvas asei d'oraisa*, a positive Torah commandment. On the last Shabbos of her life, that grandmother fulfilled a great *mitzvah,* and for all eternity, she will reap the merits of this *mitzvah* of which the doctors almost deprived her because of her minuscule quality of life.

Yafeh sha'ah achas b'teshuvah umaasim tovim b'olam hazeh mikol chayei olam haba. One hour of repentance and good deeds in this world is more precious than the entire world to come. That is how the value of life is measured according to our holy Torah.

All in the Family

THE FOLLOWING STORY REALLY HAPPENED. I HEARD IT from the *rav* in Hollywood, Florida, who was involved. A Jewish man from *Eretz Yisrael* comes to South Florida to raise money so that he would be able to marry off his daughter. He makes the rounds in Miami Beach, North Miami Beach, Fort Lauderdale, Hollywood, Hallandale and all the other Jewish communities in the area.

When he is finished, he rents a car and sets off to visit several Jewish communities along the East Coast on his way up north to New York. As he is zipping along the Interstate through the State of Georgia, he is pulled over by a state trooper for speeding.

"License and registration," says the trooper.

The man hands over the papers, and the trooper examines them carefully.

"Israel? Y'all from Israel?"

"Yes, sir."

"Well, I'm afraid I can't just write out a summons. Can't

exactly expect y'all to come back to Georgia for the hearing, can I? Y'all have to go straight to the judge right now."

Two hours later, the judge issues a fine of $175 for speeding, to be paid on the spot.

The man sighs heavily. He opens his money pouch and takes out a thick wad of cash, over $10,000. He grudgingly peels off the appropriate number of bills and hands them to the judge.

The judge's eyes bulge in astonishment. The Interstate between Florida and New York is one of the most notorious drug-trafficking routes in the United States. Surely, this man with the Israeli passport and the sack of cash must be a drug runner.

"Excuse me," says the judge, "but where did you get that money, sir?"

"I collected it," says the man.

"You collected it?" splutters the judge. "What does that mean?"

"You see, your honor, I live in Israel. I have a daughter to marry off, but I have no money. How am I going to make a wedding and buy her the things she needs to get started in life? So I came to Florida and went to different Jewish people and asked them to help me out. And that is how I collected this money."

"You expect me to believe this?" says the judge. "You come across the ocean and go to strangers and ask them to help you pay for your daughter's wedding and you come away with a sack of cash? Is that what you're telling me?"

"Almost, your honor," says the man. "They're not strangers. They're fellow Jews."

The judge shakes his head. "I'm not buying it. Unless you can come up with affidavits that you came by this money honestly, you're not going anywhere. Next case!"

In desperation, the man calls the *rav* in Hollywood, Florida, who had been very kind and helpful to him. Close to tears, he describes his predicament.

The *rav* springs into action. He collects affidavits from *rabbanim* in the different communities and faxes them to the court in Georgia. The judge is convinced, and he allows the man from Israel to continue on his way.

The state trooper, however, still finds the story too outlandish to believe. He places a telephone call to the *rav* in Hollywood, Florida.

"Let me get this straight," he says. "This guy, y'all don't know him, right?"

"That's right," said the *rav*. "Never met him before."

"He comes door to door and he asks for money?"

"That's right."

"And everybody gives him a donation?"

"Right again."

"Because he says he has a daughter in Israel that's getting married?"

"That's right."

"What's so special about this guy?"

"Nothing," says the *rav*. "We have Jewish people in need coming to us all the time. We do this all the time."

There is a brief silence on the other end of the telephone. "You know," the state trooper finally says, "I joined the wrong religion."

Speaking about choosing the wrong religion, let me tell you one more story. I take no responsibility for the veracity of this one, but its message is certainly authentic.

A Jewish man, driving along a highway in New York City, saw a car stopped by the side of the road with its hazard lights flashing. The driver, standing beside his car looking forlorn and miserable, was wearing a *yarmulke*.

A fellow Jew in distress? Time to help out. He pulled over and got out. Immediately, he noticed something was wrong. The stranded driver was indeed wearing a *yarmulke*, but he was also wearing a cross on a chain around his neck. Furthermore, from close up he looked more Hispanic than Jewish.

"What's the problem?" he said.

"Flat tire. Can you give me a hand?"

"Sure. By the way, can I ask you a question? Are you Jewish?"

The man's face broke into a grin. "Naw, I'm not Jewish. But my mother told me I should always carry a *yarmulke* in the car. And if I get stuck I should just get out of the car and put on the *yarmulke*. Someone is bound to help."

That's what Jewish people are like. We are one big family. We feel an affinity towards each other. When we look at each other, we see not strangers but brothers and sisters — or at least cousins. We are all descended from Avraham, Yitzchak and Yaakov. We try to be there for each other, because we are part of one family.

This concept which binds us together is beyond the imagination of the non-Jewish world. People like the judge and the state trooper cannot fathom such a thing.

This is not to say that non-Jews wouldn't like to belong to a broader family of people. An article in the business section of *The New York Times* told of a woman from Juneau, Alaska, who was traveling to a family get-together. As the article went on, it became clear that she would be joining some 25,000 other strangers whom she considers family. What do all these people have in common? They all bought a Saturn, a sturdy but rather prosaic little automobile built in Spring Hill, Tennessee.

Common ownership of Saturn automobiles? That constitutes family? This is the bind that ties? How desperate and pathetic.

But we're not like that. We know what it means to be family. Just like we feel an affinity and a closeness to our blood relatives who share the same gene pool, we also feel an affinity to all Jews who share the same metaphysical gene pool. In that sense, we're all related. We feel a closeness to every Jew, an automatic kinship, even if we don't even know the person.

The idea that we Jews are all one family gives us a nice, cozy feeling. It makes us feel warm inside, as we well should. But it also engenders responsibility. It means caring for another Jew as you would for your own brother, which entails more than giving him $5, $10 or $18 when he comes to the door. It means doing your part to solve the problems that are really out there, the profound problems that face every single community.

It seems to me that Jewish communities everywhere face similar problems. I once conducted an informal, decidedly unscientific survey among my colleagues in the rabbinate. I asked them to list the most serious problems their communities are facing. As I had expected, the same problems topped all their lists.

Very high on everyone's list was the problem of tuition. The cost of providing *chinuch* for their children places a tremendous burden on families everywhere. It is not uncommon for families with three or four children to spend $20,000-$30,000 a year just for elementary school education. This does not even include high school, *yeshivah gedolah* or seminary, simply the tuition for the community day school. It is a crushing burden. At the same time, the day schools, *yeshivos* and Bais Yaakovs are staggering under crushing deficits. Very often, they can't meet payrolls. *Rabbeim* and teachers in every community are overworked and underpaid. Even when they do get paid, it can be six or eight weeks late. The Orthodox Jewish community, which does not have the option of turning to public education, is overwhelmed by the problem of tuition.

This really leads us back to another problem that is very high on all lists, the general difficulty of making a living. Being an Orthodox Jew is expensive. There's tuition. There's kosher food. There's Pesach. There's summer camp. It takes a lot of money for people in the Orthodox community to make ends meet. And all too often, the ends don't quite meet.

Not long ago, General Motors announced that, for the first time in many years, they were hiring again. Moreover, they were offering high-paying jobs, as high as $17.50 an hour. This means that an automotive worker could earn $35,000-$40,000 a year. What does this mean to your average non-Jewish, blue collar worker? Heaven. He has two children in public school, buys cheap burgers and lives in an inexpensive neighborhood. Forty thousand dollars a year! He's on easy street.

But can a Jewish family with four or five children get by with $40,000? With great difficulty. Even with $60,000 or $70,000, it is exceedingly difficult. In fact, in a certain community in the New York area, a family with two children in school can make up to $120,000 and still qualify for a scholarship at the school.

So how do people cope with the problems of high tuition payments and making a living in general? They are forced to hold down more than one job or have both husband and wife work just to make ends meet. This, of course, gives rise to a new set of problems such as childcare, surrogate parenting, latchkey children, increased tension in the home and stress on the marital relationship. This is the lot of people fortunate enough to have jobs.

What about people who are underemployed? What about the people who lose their jobs? What about the person working for a major corporation that downsizes and lays him off at the ripe old age of 46 or 50?

Here he was, a highly skilled, well-paid, middle-aged successful professional, and now he's out of a job. So he tries to find a similar position and salary in the job market today, but it doesn't happen. He's out of a job for one month, two months, four months, six months, and he becomes desperate. It's not only the financial pressure, which is enormous; unemployment pays a pittance. Slowly, he becomes a different person. He begins to doubt himself. His ego is destroyed. If a man can't take care of his family, if he can't put food on the table, he sees himself as a failure. He begins to wonder what his wife thinks of him, what his children think of him. He is a broken man.

Let me just address one more problem that appeared on everyone's list: the issue of *shidduchim*. In our times, it has become incredibly hard for people to find the proper mate, and this has become a problem of immense magnitude for the entire community.

A distinguished rav once told me, "I want you to know that my daughter is my night *seder*." He has a daughter of marriageable age, and every night, for the entire night, he is busy with her *shidduchim*. He is constantly on the phone making calls to people, trying to get people to suggest a good *shidduch*, finding out about the boys that do come his way, about their families. This is what occupies his mind.

I recently met a friend from my *yeshivah* days. We exchanged a few pleasantries. Then he said to me, "Every morning, before I say Modeh Ani, I ask myself, what am I doing for my daughter today?" It has obviously become an obsession.

If this is the situation with those boys and girls fortunate enough to have parents who think and worry about them, how much worse is it for those who do not?

What about the hundreds and hundreds of boys and girls that, for whatever reason, do not have parents to worry about them? What about those that don't have parents to make the calls at night, who don't know the rules of the game?

What about the men and women, girls who are already older, who see their classmates all getting married? What about those who see the many hundreds of aging singles and feel the awful fear that *shidduchim* will pass them by?

And what about the aging singles themselves, who are no longer 23 and 24 but 34 and 38? What about these poor souls who feel lost and abandoned in our family-oriented society?

Over the years, I have received a number of letters on

these subjects, and I would like to quote excerpts from three of them. Marketing experts contend that every letter a company receives, whether complaint or compliment, represents 35 letters that other people wanted to send but didn't have the time or the patience. By their count, these three letters represent at least a hundred people with similar stories, and I have no doubt that the number is far, far greater.

"Rabbi, for the sake of all Jewish mothers and grandmothers, fathers and grandfathers, please hear me out," writes one single woman. "So many single men and women need help. We need the community to help us. I have dealt with professionals, but to no avail. I beg you to start some kind of movement. Many in the singles community feel a sense of abandonment by the Jewish community. Can't we have professional people working solely for helping the Jewish community produce healthy and productive couples?"

Here is another letter. "It seems to me that there are more girls than boys," writes a woman from Montreal. "When we get a name of a good *bachur*, our daughter's name is just on a big list. And if she's not from New York, it's almost a lost cause. We get excuses that boys don't want to come so far when there are plenty of girls in New York. So we have sent our daughters to New York. They have to live in an apartment and find jobs. This is not a way of life for a Jewish girl. Our daughters are miserable. They are embarrassed to go to *shul*. In our society, a girl of 23 is considered an old maid, and everyone pities her. We mothers are so sad to see our daughters distressed and unhappy. Our walls are the only witnesses that hear our cries."

Finally, there is this letter from a divorced mother bringing up two children on her own. "Several months ago," she writes, "I felt abandoned by those people who should have helped me find employment. Unfortunately, many divorced or widowed women suffer the abandonment in our community. Many people seem to think that widowhood or a bad marriage is like a contagious virus. If you come too close, you may catch it."

These are all extremely serious problems with which our community must contend. There are no simple solutions, and it is certainly not my intention here to offer global strategies and suggestions to the community at large. Still, I would like to make a few comments on the subject.

I believe that before any solutions can be formulated and implemented, there must be a fundamental shift in our attitudes towards our fellow Jews. If we really believe that we are all one family, then the problems of our fellow Jews are actually our own problems.

Therefore, even those of us who have ample income, who pay full tuition without difficulty, whose children are much sought after or already married, who are enjoying a blessed existence, even those people must feel personally troubled and agitated by the distress of their fellow Jews. If your next-door neighbor is out of a job, it has to be your problem. You can't just shake your head and cluck your tongue. You have to do something.

In his introduction to *Sefer Shaarei Yosher*, Rav Shimon Shkop discusses a paradox about the human condition. All of us are preoccupied with ourselves. From the moment of birth, each of us is already thinking about only one person, himself. A hungry baby who cries in the night is thinking only about himself. It is how we're made; it is our nature. We are all motivated by self-love, by an overriding preoccupation with the self. And yet, observes Rav Shimon, every Jew has a responsibility to be concerned about others. How can we reconcile this anomaly? How can we bridge the gap between preoccupation with the self and concern for others?

The only way, explains Rav Shimon, is to progressively redefine the parameters of self. At the most primitive level, a person's definition of self includes no other people at all. When a person rises to a higher level, his definition of the self expands to include his wife, his children, his parents, his grandchildren, and so on. The truly great person, however, redefines his concept of self to include not only himself, not only his family, not only his friends, but the entire community, all the Jewish people. That is how we can bridge the gap.

In this light, Rav Shimon explains the *mishnah* in *Avos*. "If I am not for myself, who will be for me?" If a person doesn't take responsibility for himself, if he doesn't care about himself, who else will? Granted, there has to be concern for the self. But, the *mishnah* goes on, "If I am for myself, what am I?" But if a person worries only about himself, his wife, his children, what is he? A pathetic excuse for a human being.

This, in a nutshell, is what distinguishes our *gedolim* from the rest of us. They have reached a level of development where their self is all-inclusive. They no longer differentiate between their own needs and the needs of others. Their instinct for self-preservation drives them to care for others.

At the turn of the 20th century, a fire ravaged the city of Brisk. Fully half of the dwellings were destroyed, and numerous Jewish people were left homeless. During this calamity, Rav Chaim Soloveitchik , the Rav of Brisk, refused to sleep in his own home. Instead, he slept in a small room off the *shul*.

"Please come sleep in your own bed," his family begged him. "What you're doing is ruining your health."

"How can I sleep in a bed," Rav Chaim replied, "when half the people of the city don't have roofs over their heads?"

That's a *gadol*.

Most of us are not on that level. If a neighbor's house should burn down, Heaven forbid, we would not feel compelled to abandon our own comfortable beds. But we should at least be on the level to care about it. We should at least be out there offering our neighbor food and shelter and an encouraging word. We should find it within ourselves to include our stricken neighbor, at least to some extent, in our broader definition of self.

The same holds true if we hear about a lawyer or an

accountant or a computer consultant who lost his job. It is not enough simply to shake our heads in sympathy and say, "Hey, that's a tough break, but something else is bound to come up." You know other lawyers. You have business associates that may be able to use the services of a good accountant or computer consultant. You have contacts and connections. Get on the telephone and make a few calls. If you really care, do something. Pick up the telephone.

When someone asks you if you can suggest a *shidduch* for their son or daughter, listen with an open mind. Sure, it's easy to beg off, and there are dozens of excuses to help you get out of it. Sure, you don't know the boy or the girl so well. Sure, you don't want the responsibility. But you can still make an effort, a real effort. If you make the call and get the answering machine, that doesn't let you off the hook. If you leave a message, and they don't return the call, that doesn't let you off the hook.

What if it were your own daughter? When it comes to our own children we spare no effort. We have to make the effort for other people's children. After all, their children are our children. Include others in your expanded self, and you'll look at their needs in an entirely different light.

I heard about a woman who started something called a *shidduch* club in her neighborhood. Once a month, the ladies put their heads together to try to find *shidduchim* for people in the community, and it works. We are a creative people. If we put our minds to it, there is nothing we cannot accomplish.

Rav Sholom Schwadron once saw a little child fall down in the street in Yerushalayim. The child was cut and bleeding profusely. Rav Sholom scooped the child into his arms and set off at a run towards the hospital.

An old lady witnessed the scene from a distance. "Don't run!" she called out to Rav Sholom as he ran past her. "Don't worry. Everything will be all right. Hashem will help."

Suddenly, she took a closer look at the child and realized

it was her own grandchild. She began to wring her hands and scream hysterically. "Faster, faster! Get him to the hospital."

When it was her own grandchild, the calm assurance and sanctimonious *bitachon* suddenly disappeared.

Even if you are unsuccessful in helping others find *shidduchim*, you can undoubtedly help simply by offering them your hospitality. Invite a lonely person for a Shabbos or a Yom Tov meal. Show them that your door is always open to them. It makes a tremendous difference.

A friend of mine who lives in Brooklyn rents out his basement apartment to a single fellow, a learned man whose marriage had failed. My friend would exchange a few pleasantries with his tenant from time to time, but otherwise had very little contact with him.

One Friday night, my friend and his wife threw a birthday party for one of their children. They invited the family, gave out treats to the children and sang a few songs. After the children went off to play, the adults sat around drinking tea and making small talk.

While they were talking, they heard the downstairs tenant singing *zemiros*. On a sudden impulse, my friend's wife decided to invite the tenant to come up and join the family for a little tea and conversation. The man gratefully accepted. He drank a cup of tea, ate a few cookies and joined in the conversation. After a half-hour, he bid everyone a good Shabbos and went back to his basement apartment.

After Shabbos, he approached my friend. "I want to tell you something," he said. "I had decided that this was my last observant Shabbos. I was completely fed up with eating alone Friday nights, staring at the four walls and singing *zemiros* all by myself. I was through. This was it. But then you invited me up, and I decided that I wasn't going to give it up after all."

There's a happy ending to this story. The man is now remarried, and he has a beautiful family. And why? Because someone had the impulse to invite this lonely man for tea and small talk on a Friday night.

Each and every one of us can help a person in distress in one way or another. All it takes is a little sensitivity. Even if there is nothing practical we can do, even if we have no contacts to turn to, absolutely no *shidduchim* to suggest, we can still extend a hand in friendship. We can still lend a sympathetic ear and simply listen.

The simple act of listening is therapeutic. And we can all do it. All it takes is a little time and patience. Not to listen to a person who wants to unburden himself is inexcusable.

The Gemara (*Shabbos* 55a) relates that Rav Yehudah was sitting in the *beis din* next to Shmuel, his *rebbi*. A woman came in and started pouring out the miseries in her heart to Shmuel, but Shmuel remained sitting impassively.

"Why doesn't the *rebbi* answer her?" Rav Yehudah asked Shmuel. "Didn't we learn (*Mishlei* 21:12) that 'whoever shuts his ears to the cries of the downtrodden will not be answered when he himself calls for help'?"

"It's not for me to respond to her," Shmuel replied, "since Mar Ukva is here and this *beis din* is under his jurisdiction."

Elsewhere, the Gemara (*Bava Basra* 10a) mentions that an Amora went up to Heaven and saw an inverted world. People considered "lower" in this world had a higher station than their superiors in Heaven. Tosefos explains in the name of Rabbeinu Chananel that this refers to Shmuel and Rav Yehudah. In this world, Shmuel enjoyed a higher station than Rav Yehudah, but in Heaven Rav Yehudah stood higher. Why? Because Rav Yehudah wanted Shmuel to listen to the distraught woman even though he lacked the authority to do anything practical for her in Mar Ukva's *beis din*. And he was right. You have to listen, even if you can't do anything.

Many years ago, a *talmid* of Rav Yitzchak Hutner, a young man learning in *kollel*, had a child with very serious medical problems. He poured out his heart to Rav Hutner, and as he spoke, he was so overcome by his misfortune that he broke down and sat there crying. Embarrassed, he covered his face with his hands until he could regain his composure. When he finally looked up, he saw tears streaming down Rav Hutner's face. To this day, he remembers this moment with a warm feeling. Rav Hutner gave him no advice, no guidance. But he listened. He cared.

Some time ago, on a cold and dark winter morning, my teenaged son woke me before dawn to tell me he was having severe stomach cramps. I suggested he drink some flat cola, but it didn't help. I went to his room and sat with him as he lay writhing in pain on his bed.

Fifteen minutes later, my wife came into the room. She tried helping him by telling him to lie on his stomach. When that didn't help, she suggested he lie on his back.

Soon after, my daughter came in. She also had suggestions. Try standing up and walking around. Take some Pepto Bismol. Everyone had advice. Nothing helped.

At 9 o'clock, he wasn't getting better, and I called the doctor. By 9:30, we were in the emergency room. By 10 o'clock, we were out of the emergency room on the way home. It was nothing major, just a reaction to an antibiotic he was taking.

I remember sitting thinking about that early morning in my son's room. All that useless advice. What had we done for him? His stomach cramps were not subsiding. But in truth, we had done a lot for him. We were there for him. His mother, his father, his sister, we were all there. He was in the warm embrace of his family, and that is a wonderful comfort.

One final point. From a metaphysical standpoint, there is one more thing we can do for our fellow Jews even if we cannot help in a practical way, even if we listen but it doesn't help. The Alter of Kelm points out that if Hashem sees Jews trying to help each other, even if they are ineffective, He is inspired, so to speak, to extend a helping hand from Heaven.

When Moshe first went out to see how his Jewish brethren were faring, Rashi writes that "*nasan einav velibo ... aleihem.*" Moshe turned his eyes and heart to the condition of his fellow Jews. Later, when Hashem takes note of the suffering of the Jewish people, Rashi writes that "*nasan aleihem leiv*." Hashem turned His heart to them. The Alter of Kelm is struck by the similarity of the phrasing. What does it signify?

There is a concept in Kabbalah, the Alter explains, called *is'arusa delesata* and *is'arusa dele'eila*. An awakening in the lower world can inspire an awakening Above. Some problems may be beyond our scope and ability. Nonetheless, if we really make the effort, if we awaken in our hearts a passionate desire to help our fellow Jews, we can inspire a new awakening in Heaven. When Moshe's heart went out to his enslaved brethren, Hashem also took pity on them and "remembered" their plight.

We can "prevail" on Hashem, the One Who provides livelihoods to one and all, the One Who brings together husband and wife, to take pity on our fellow Jews who are suffering. Nothing is beyond His scope and capability. If he sees that we care, that we are making the effort, He will make it happen — even if it takes a miracle.

Let me end with another letter I received from the woman in Montreal who was having difficulty finding a *shidduch* for her daughter. One day, I checked my mailbox and found an invitation from Montreal. I didn't recognize the name. I opened the invitation and there was a note from this very mother.

"My daughter has become a *kallah*," she informed me joyously. "I have a feeling it was more than my *tefillos* and the *tefillos* of other people. You see, I have been trying to get something going in my community, to help people find *shidduchim*. Maybe Hashem responded by helping me find a *shidduch* for my daughter."

This is exactly what the Alter of Kelm was saying. If we try, if we make the effort, if we show Hashem that we care, He will open His hand and give sustenance to those who lack, send life mates to those who suffer in loneliness and perhaps even send all of us *Mashiach* to bring this long exile to an end.

Thank You, Rebbitzen Shapiro

DAF YOMI. IT IS A MOVEMENT THAT HAS SWEPT THE world. It is a word that every child knows. Learning the daily *daf* has become almost as ingrained in our daily routine as our daily *tefillos*. Practically every *shul* has a well-attended daily *Daf Yomi shiur*. We have *Daf* on the Long Island Railroad, a special car set aside for a daily *shiur* for commuters. *Daf Yomi shiurim* are readily available on Dial-a-Daf call-in lines, audiocassettes and interactive CD-ROMS. They are even piped in to the sound systems on El Al flights. Many tens of thousands of people filled both Madison Square Garden and Nassau Coliseum for the last Siyum Hashas.

A world without *Daf Yomi* is unimaginable to us, yet one century ago it did not exist. Just over one century ago, the founder of the *Daf Yomi* movement, Rav Meir Shapiro, the Lubliner Rav, was just a little boy.

In the year 1894, on *Isru Chag* Pesach, when young Meir Shapiro was only 7 years old, he saw that his mother was crying.

"*Mamme,* why are you crying?" he asked.

"Because your *melamed* did not come today," she replied. "He was supposed to come today, but he is not here yet."

"So why are you crying?"

"You don't understand, Meir'l. You are too young. If you miss a day of learning, it can never be replaced."

This answer penetrated deep into his heart, and when he grew up, it became one of the fundamental ideals of the *Daf Yomi* movement. *Daf Yomi* is about the constancy of learning. The consistency of doing something day in day out, year in and year out over the span of an entire lifetime.

We find a discussion in the *Midrash* as to which *passuk* best exemplifies the essence of Torah.

Ben Zoma claims that the essence of Torah is encapsulated by the words, "*Shema Yisrael, Hashem Elokeinu, Hashem echad.* Hear, O Israel, Hashem is our Lord, Hashem is One."

Ben Nannes claims that the essence of Torah is encapsulated by the words, "*Ve'ahavta lerei'acha kamocha.* Love your fellow as you love yourself."

Ben Pazi claims that the essence of Torah is encapsulated by the words, "*Es hakeves echad taaseh baboker, ve'es hakeves hasheini taaseh bein ha'arbayim.* You shall prepare the first lamb [for the daily *Korban Tamid*] in the morning and the second lamb in the evening."

Rebbi rose and declared, "Ben Pazi is right!"

Let us take a moment to consider this perplexing *Midrash.* We can readily understand Ben Zoma's choice of *Shema Yisrael* as the embodiment of the Torah. It reiterates *Kabbalas Ol Malchus Shamayim,* the submission to the sovereignty of the Kingdom of Heaven, which is the basis of the relationship between a person and his Creator, *bein adam laMakom.*

We can also understand Ben Nannes's choice of *Ve'ahavta lerei'acha kamocha* as the essence of Torah, since this forms the basis of a person's relationship with others, *bein adam lachaveiro.*

But how are we to understand Ben Pazi's choice of the *Korban Tamid* as representative of the essence of Torah? And how are we to understand Rebbi's endorsement of this point of view?

The Maharal explains that the essential prerequisite of Torah, of being a true servant of Hashem, is consistency. Torah is a commitment, day in day out, every single day. The Torah is constancy, like the *Korban Tamid.* And that is what *Daf Yomi* is all about: constancy, commitment, dedication. It doesn't really matter if it is a daily *daf*, a daily *amud*, a daily *mishnah.* Daily is the operative word. That is the spirit of *Daf Yomi.* A day is irreplaceable.

Rav Meir Shapiro was a man of incredibly broad vision, and it is no surprise that *Daf Yomi,* his brainchild, is as versatile and complex as its creator. One of his primary goals in proposing *Daf Yomi* was to form a unifying factor, a common denominator that would be shared by widely disparate groups in the Jewish community. Daf Yomi was intended to promote *achdus,* national unity, among the Jewish people. And if a stimulus for unity was needed 75 years ago, how much greater is the need today when we have become so fragmented.

When Balak summoned Bilaam to curse the Jewish people, he showed him the outer edges of the Jewish encampment and said, "You will see but a part of the nation, but you will not see all of it." The commentators are puzzled. If Bilaam was supposed to curse the Jewish people, Heaven forbid, wouldn't it have made sense to show him the entire encampment?

The Skulener Rebbe zatzal explains that an enemy can only attack fragmented parts of the Jewish people, those parts that are isolated from the main body of the Jewish people by divisiveness and disunity. But if the Jewish people are together, in a unified state, they are invincible.

Daf Yomi has been one of the main forces for unity among the Jewish people over the last half century. Countless thousands of people from all walks of life and from every stripe of Orthodoxy spend a significant portion of every day on the same page, literally and figuratively. What better basis of unity can there be than having the same Talmudic questions and issues occupy our minds every single day? Because of *Daf Yomi,* we are indeed unified, with one goal and one aspiration. We are united by Torah and for Torah, and that makes us strong and invulnerable.

Furthermore, if we think into it, we will discover that *Daf Yomi* also fosters unity on an entirely different level. Not only does *Daf Yomi* unite people from different walks of life, it also adds unity and structure to our personal lives.

The Gemara in *Pesachim* (68) tells us that Rav Yosef declared, "If not for the day of *Kabalas HaTorah,* there would be many Yosefs in the marketplace."

My *rosh yeshivah*, Rav Yaakov Yitzchak Halevi Ruderman used to say, *al pi drush*, that these "many Yosefs" are not actually different people but rather different facets of the same person. People do indeed have many sides to them. Speaking in the context of today's world, a person may be active in the business or professional world for part of the day, a *shtiebel Yid* for another part of the day and a devoted father and husband for yet a third part of the day. All of these sides of his personality are legitimate aspects of who he is. But what brings them all together? What unifies these disparate parts into one harmonious whole? It is the Torah. When a person makes the Torah the focus of his life, all the other parts of his persona become integrated into this one transcendent whole. Therefore, if not for Torah, there would be many different Yosefs in the marketplace, but the Torah brings them all together.

Daf Yomi has brought a steady stream of Torah into innumerable lives and as such has been the great unifier of individual souls and lives.

If we think back for a moment to that scene in the childhood of Rav Meir Shapiro that planted the seed of Daf Yomi in his brain, we gain yet another insight into the meaning of Daf Yomi. The importance of learning Torah every single day without exception was conveyed by none other than his mother, by his Yiddishe mamme, one of a legion of Yiddishe mammes. These valiant women have always been the guardians of the fountainhead of Torah. Their tears, their prayers and their efforts have ensured that the flow of Torah would not be interrupted.

Today, as well, it is the support of the women that is responsible for the phenomenal growth of the Torah world. Daf Yomi is made possible by women who encourage their husbands to learn and excel and continue to grow. They reap the benefits, because there can be no greater assurance of the spiritual well-being of a Jewish home than a husband who learns Torah.

Sometimes this requires sacrifice on the part of the woman of the house. It is not unusual for a husband to come home after a long day at work, grab a few bites of supper, spend some time helping the children with their homework, and then it's off to the Daf Yomi shiur. The wife is left to cope with dinner, homework, baths, bedtime, and all the rest. This is sacrifice. Or the scenario can take place in the morning, during those hectic hours when the children must be prepared for the day and sent off to school. Often a wife feels that another pair of hands and another person would be so incredibly helpful, but her husband has left for his Daf Yomi shiur at 5:30 or 6 in the morning. This is sacrifice, and for this, the women deserve all the credit.

Rav Meir Shapiro's mother paid her son's melamed the unheard of sum of 300 rubles. Why? "Es iz a kleine korban far aza groisse Torah," she would say. "It is a small sacrifice to make for such a great Torah." The women are prepared to make the sacrifice, and that is why we have such a wealth of Torah in our world today.

With his *Daf Yomi,* Rav Meir Shapiro has also taught us a tangential but extremely important lesson. He has taught that a single person armed with a powerful vision and boundless dedication can make a tremendous difference in this world. Rav Meir Shapiro had an idea, an incredible idea, and he acted on it. Look at the result! Look at all the millions of hours and *dafim* that have been learned because of one idea and one man, a man who lived in our century.

True, Rav Meir Shapiro was a genius and a great *gadol.* But in actuality, even ordinary people can make a difference with one stroke. In fact, sometimes they can make a difference without even knowing about it.

I once heard a story about a Jewish man who approached a rabbi in Dallas, Texas, and gave him $10,000.

"What's this all about?" asked the rabbi.

"Well, you see, Rabbi, I was at the Western Wall, and I saw this religious fellow, one of those Jerusalem people with the long coat and the flying earlocks and the straggly beard, if you get the picture. Well, this fellow was praying like I never saw anybody pray. Such concentration. Such intensity. I've never seen anything like it. I like what I saw, and I want to be part of that world. I want you to give this $10,000 to Orthodox causes. And I'm going to give you another $10,000 every year for as long as I live."

And this was exactly what the man did until the day he died. After he died, his old mother continued the tradition of giving the yearly $10,000 until she passed away.

Imagine what that one Yerushalmi at the *Kosel* accomplished with that one *tefillah* with *kavanah.* When he comes up to the Heavenly Court, he will be shown all the *yeshivos* he supported and all the orphaned brides he helped marry off.

"When and where did I do these things?" he will ask, bewildered.

"It was through the Jewish man from Dallas," he will be told.

"Which Jewish man from Dallas? I've never been to Dallas. I never even heard of Dallas."

It won't matter. He will get the *sechar*. Because of his one deed, he will be given eternal reward in boundless measure. Whether it is a great *gadol* like Rav Meir Shapiro instituting *Daf Yomi* or an ordinary Jew with a heartfelt Minchah at the *Kosel*, there is no limit to what one act by one person can accomplish.